Historic Poems and Ballads

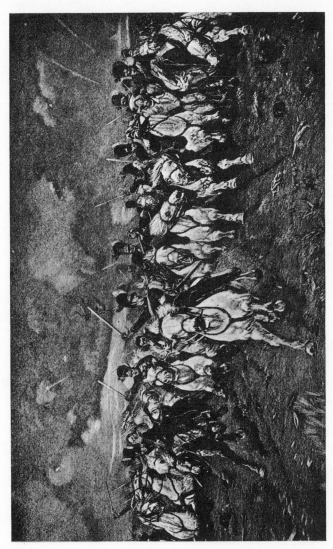

CHARGE OF THE SCOTCH GREYS AT WATERLOO

Historic Poems and Ballads

Described by
RUPERT S. HOLLAND

Granger Index Reprint Series

BOOKS FOR LIBRARIES PRESS
FREEPORT, NEW YORK

First Published 1912
Reprinted 1970

STANDARD BOOK NUMBER:
8369-6147-1

LIBRARY OF CONGRESS CATALOG CARD NUMBER:
75-116406

MANUFACTURED
BY
HALLMARK LITHOGRAPHERS, INC.
IN THE U.S.A.

Contents

6 CONTENTS

CONTENTS

Illustrations

I

The Destruction of Sennacherib

SENNACHERIB was King of Assyria from 705 B. C. to 681 B. C. He was a very proud and warlike ruler, but also a great builder, and during his reign Assyria became famous for her art and architecture. He seized and destroyed Babylon, conquered Chaldea, and marched into Egypt. City after city of Judah fell before his arms, and Hezekiah, Prince of Judah, was forced to retreat into Jerusalem. The Assyrian king pursued, wasting the land with fire and sword, and taking the people for slaves. As Sennacherib swept up to Jerusalem the Prince of Judah tried to ransom his city with gold, but the invader would not listen to his offer, and prepared to attack the walls. Then suddenly a plague fell upon the great Assyrian host. It is said that 185,000 men died in a single night. The rest, terrified at what seemed retribution for their destruction of Babylon, fled in a panic, pursued by their enemies. The king himself escaped, but was killed in 681 B. C. in the temple at Nineveh by two of his sons.

Byron wrote a number of poems dealing with Hebrew history, and this is one of the most spirited of them. It describes how the great Assyrian army, flushed with scores of victories, came to Jerusalem, ready to conquer on the morrow. That night came the plague, and the army melted away before its breath. The widows of Ashur, which means Assyria, bewailed the lost soldiers, and the priests who tended the altars of the god Baal broke the idols in despair, for the Gentiles, or heathens, who had been so powerful before, had fallen, not by men's swords, but at the will of the God of Jerusalem.

THE DESTRUCTION OF SENNACHERIB
By George Gordon Noel, Lord Byron

The Assyrian came down like the wolf on the fold,
And his cohorts were gleaming in purple and gold ;
And the sheen of their spears was like stars on the sea,
When the blue wave rolls nightly on deep Galilee.

Like the leaves of the forest when summer is green,
That host with their banners at sunset were seen ;
Like the leaves of the forest when autumn hath flown,
That host on the morrow lay withered and strown.

For the angel of death spread his wings on the blast,
And breathed in the face of the foe as he passed ;
And the eyes of the sleepers waxed deadly and chill,
And their hearts but once heaved, and forever grew still !

And there lay the steed with his nostril all wide,
But through it there rolled not the breath of his pride ;
And the foam of his gasping lay white on the turf,
And cold as the spray of the rock-beating surf.

And there lay the rider distorted and pale,
With the dew on his brow and the rust on his mail ;
And the tents were all silent, the banners alone,
The lances unlifted, the trumpet unblown.

And the widows of Ashur are loud in their wail;
And the idols are broke in the temple of Baal;
And the might of the Gentile, unsmote by the sword,
Hath melted like snow in the glance of the Lord !

II

Horatius

THIS poem gives such a true picture of the patriotic spirit of a citizen of early Rome, and follows the metre of many Latin poets so closely that it might well have been what Macaulay pretended it was, a lay actually written about three hundred and sixty years after the founding of Rome, or in 393 B. C.

At that time the most powerful chief in Italy was Lars Porsena, of Etruria, whose capital city was Clusium, which was some ninety miles to the north-west of Rome. Etruria was the home of the twelve Etruscan tribes, and lay to the north and west of Rome, separated from that city by the river Tiber. Among the Etruscans the word *Lars* meant *lord* or *chief*. Like the Romans the Etruscans had a number of gods, to each of whom they ascribed different attributes, as the Romans did to Jupiter, Minerva, Mars, and their other deities.

Rome had been a kingdom at one time, and its kings had come from the house of Tarquin. But Tarquin the Proud had ruled so tyrannously, and his son, "false Sextus," had committed so vile a crime, that the people had overthrown his power and driven Tarquin from the city in 505 B. C. He had sought aid from Lars Porsena, and that chief, already jealous of Rome's prosperity, determined to raise a great army and replace Tarquin on his throne.

The Etruscan chieftain sent out his messengers, and soon had gathered allies from the twelve tribes. They came from all central Italy, from the fastnesses of the Apennine Mountains, from the city of Volaterræ whose citadel was made of huge uncemented boulders, from Populonia, opposite the island of Sardinia, from the busy city of Pisa, in whose harbor were triremes, or ships with triple-banks of oars, belonging to the colony of Massilia in Gaul, from the country watered by the river Clanis, and from the many-towered city of Cortona. The woodmen left the forests that lay along the river Auser, the hunters deserted the stags of the Ciminian hill in Etruria, the herdsmen forsook the milk-white cattle that browsed on the banks of the stream Clitumnus. The Volsinian lake was left in peace to its water fowl, old men reaped the harvests in Arretium, young boys cared for the sheep-shearing along the Umbro, and in the city of Luna girls pressed the grapes in the wine-vats while their fathers joined the march to Rome.

Meantime Lars Porsena took counsel with his soothsayers, and they consulted the books, in which was supposed to be written, from right to left, according to the Etruscan fashion, the future of that nation. The thirty wise men assured him that he would conquer and bring back to his own capital the shields of Rome.

The great army of Etruscans, 80,000 footmen and 10,000 horsemen, gathered before the gates of Sutrium. Enemies of Rome, men who had been banished from that city, and Mamilius, Prince of Latium, a country south of Rome, came to join the soldiers of Etruria.

In Rome there was great dismay. The farmers who lived in the open country drove their cattle, and carried their household goods, inside the city walls. From the high Tarpeian Rock the people could see the blazing towns fired by Lars Porsena on his march. The Senate of the city sat night and day, and every hour new messengers arrived with word of the enemy's advance. As they advanced the Etruscans destroyed all hostile settlements, they leveled Crustumerium, a town in the Sabine country that belonged to Rome; Verbenna, one of their generals, swept across to the port of Ostia, at the mouth of the Tiber; and Astur, another leader, captured the fortified hill of Janiculum that lay across the Tiber to the west of Rome. That hill commanded the only bridge that spanned the river, and if the Etruscans should seize it they would probably soon break a way into the city.

The Consul, who was one of the chief officers of Rome, ordered the bridge destroyed, but at the same moment a messenger brought word that Lars Porsena was in sight. The Consul looked and saw the glittering line of spears and helmets, the banners of the twelve chief cities of Etruria, and the leaders themselves.

The Consul saw that the enemy were so close that their vanguard would prevent the Romans destroying the bridge in time. But even as he said this Horatius, the Captain of the Gate, stepped forward, and volunteered to hold the enemy in check, if two others would fight beside him. Instantly two brave men offered

HORATIUS AT THE BRIDGE

to go forth, the one Spurius Lartius, and the other Herminius.

The three Romans armed and stepped forward to the other bank of the Tiber, while the Consul, the City Fathers, and citizens seized hatchets and crowbars, and began to loosen the supports of the bridge.

The Etruscan army saw the three Romans standing at the head of the bridge, and thought it would be a simple matter to overcome them. Three chiefs rushed forward, only to fall before the swords of Horatius and his allies. More tried it, and more, but each in turn met the same fate before the Romans. At last the great Etruscan army stood at bay.

Time had been gained for the people to destroy the props of the bridge. As it began to fall, the Romans called to their three defenders. Spurius Lartius and Herminius dashed back, but Horatius was left on the other shore when the bridge crashed into the river.

Horatius would not yield, but with a prayer to Father Tiber plunged into the stream. While all eyes watched him he swam to the Roman bank. There the people raised him on their shoulders and carried him in triumph through the city gates.

Rome gave its hero a section of the public lands, and built a statue of him in the Forum. The story of how Horatius held the bridge became one of the great chronicles of Rome.

Macaulay's greatest work was his " History of England." His poems were written as recreation from heavier work, but in " Horatius" he composed one of the most vivid and stirring historical poems in the

English language. It is a remarkable example of the
power of direct narrative, and gains much of its force
from the short, simple words and plain recital of events
as if seen by the narrator.

HORATIUS

By Thomas Babbington, Lord Macaulay

(A Lay made about the Year of the City CCCLX.)

I

Lars Porsena of Clusium
  By the Nine Gods he swore
That the great house of Tarquin
  Should suffer wrong no more.
By the Nine Gods he swore it,
  And named a trysting day,
And bade his messengers ride forth,
East and west and south and north,
  To summon his array.

II

East and west and south and north
  The messengers ride fast,
And tower and town and cottage
  Have heard the trumpet's blast.
Shame on the false Etruscan
  Who lingers in his home
When Porsena of Clusium
  Is on the march for Rome.

III

The horsemen and the footmen
  Are pouring in amain,
From many a stately market-place;
  From many a fruitful plain;

From many a lonely hamlet,
  Which, hid by beech and pine,
Like an eagle's nest, hangs on the crest
  Of purple Apennine;

IV

From lordly Volaterræ,
  Where scowls the far-famed hold
Piled by the hands of giants
  For godlike kings of old;
From sea-girt Populonia,
  Whose sentinels descry
Sardinia's snowy mountain-tops
  Fringing the southern sky;

V

From the proud mart of Pisæ,
  Queen of the western waves,
Where ride Massilia's triremes
  Heavy with fair-haired slaves;
From where sweet Clanis wanders
  Through corn and vines and flowers;
From where Cortona lifts to heaven
  Her diadem of towers.

VI

Tall are the oaks whose acorns
  Drop in dark Auser's rill;
Fat are the stags that champ the boughs
  Of the Ciminian hill;
Beyond all streams Clitumnus
  Is to the herdsman dear;
Best of all pools the fowler loves
  The great Volsinian mere.

VII

But now no stroke of woodman
   Is heard by Auser's rill;
No hunter tracks the stag's green path
   Up the Ciminian hill;
Unwatched along Clitumnus
   Grazes the milk-white steer;
Unharmed the water fowl may dip
   In the Volsinian mere.

VIII

The harvests of Arretium,
   This year, old men shall reap,
This year, young boys in Umbro
   Shall plunge the struggling sheep;
And in the vats of Luna,
   This year, the must shall foam
Round the white feet of laughing girls
   Whose sires have marched to Rome.

IX

There be thirty chosen prophets,
   The wisest of the land,
Who alway by Lars Porsena
   Both morn and evening stand:
Evening and morn the Thirty
   Have turned the verses o'er,
Traced from the right on linen white
   By mighty seers of yore.

X

And with one voice the Thirty
   Have their glad answer given;
" Go forth, go forth, Lars Porsena;
   Go forth, beloved of Heaven;

Go, and return in glory
  To Clusium's royal dome ;
And hang round Nursia's altars
  The golden shields of Rome."

XI

And now hath every city
  Sent up her tale of men ;
The foot are fourscore thousand,
  The horse are thousands ten.
Before the gates of Sutrium
  Is met the great array.
A proud man was Lars Porsena
  Upon the trysting day.

XII

For all the Etruscan armies
  Were ranged beneath his eye,
And many a banished Roman,
  And many a stout ally ;
And with a mighty following
  To join the muster came
The Tusculan Mamilius,
  Prince of the Latian name.

XIII

But by the yellow Tiber
  Was tumult and affright :
From all the spacious champaign
  To Rome men took their flight.
A mile around the city,
  The throng stopped up the ways ;
A fearful sight it was to see
  Through two long nights and days.

XIV

For droves of mules and asses
  Laden with skins of wine,
And endless flocks of goats and sheep,
  And endless herds of kine,
And endless trains of wagons
  That creaked beneath the weight
Of corn-sacks and of household goods,
  Choked every roaring gate.

XV

Now, from the rock Tarpeian,
  Could the wan burghers spy
The line of blazing villages
  Red in the midnight sky.
The Fathers of the City,
  They sat all night and day,
For every hour some horseman came
  With tidings of dismay.

XVI

To eastward and to westward
  Have spread the Tuscan bands;
Nor house, nor fence, nor dovecot
  In Crustumerium stands.
Verbenna down to Ostia
  Hath wasted all the plain;
Astur hath stormed Janiculum,
  And the stout guards are slain.

XVII

I wis, in all the Senate,
  There was no heart so bold,
But sore it ached, and fast it beat,
  When that ill news was told.

Forthwith up rose the Consul,
  Up rose the Fathers all;
In haste they girded up their gowns,
  And hied them to the wall.

XVIII

They held a council standing
  Before the River-Gate;
Short time was there, ye well may guess,
  For musing or debate.
Out spake the Consul roundly:
  "The bridge must straight go down;
For, since Janiculum is lost,
  Naught else can save the town."

XIX

Just then a scout came flying,
  All wild with haste and fear:
"To arms! to arms! Sir Consul:
  Lars Porsena is here."
On the low hills to westward
  The Consul fixed his eye,
And saw the swarthy storm of dust
  Rise fast along the sky.

XX

And nearer fast and nearer
  Doth the red whirlwind come;
And louder still and still more loud,
From underneath that rolling cloud,
Is heard the trumpet's war-note proud,
  The trampling and the hum.
And plainly and more plainly

Now through the gloom appears,
Far to left and far to right,
In broken gleams of dark-blue light,
The long array of helmets bright,
The long array of spears.

XXI

And plainly and more plainly,
Above that glimmering line,
Now might ye see the banners
Of twelve fair cities shine;
But the banner of proud Clusium
Was highest of them all,
The terror of the Umbrian,
The terror of the Gaul.

XXII

And plainly and more plainly
Now might the burghers know,
By port and vest, by horse and crest,
Each warlike Lucumo.
There Cilnius of Arretium
On his fleet roan was seen;
And Astur of the fourfold shield,
Girt with the brand none else may wield,
Tolumnius with the belt of gold,
And dark Verbenna from the hold
By reedy Thrasymene.

XXIII

Fast by the royal standard,
O'erlooking all the war,
Lars Porsena of Clusium
Sat in his ivory car.

By the right wheel rode Mamilius,
    Prince of the Latian name ;
And by the left false Sextus,
    That wrought the deed of shame.

XXIV

But when the face of Sextus
    Was seen among the foes,
A yell that rent the firmament
    From all the town arose.
On the housetops was no woman
    But spat towards him and hissed,
No child but screamed out curses,
    And shook its little fist.

XXV

But the Consul's brow was sad,
    And the Consul's speech was low,
And darkly looked he at the wall,
    And darkly at the foe.
"Their van will be upon us
    Before the bridge goes down ;
And if they once may win the bridge,
    What hope to save the town ? "

XXVI

Then out spake brave Horatius,
    The Captain of the Gate :
" To every man upon this earth
    Death cometh soon or late.
And how can man die better
    Than facing fearful odds,
For the ashes of his fathers,
    And the temples of his Gods,

XXVII

" And for the tender mother
    Who dandled him to rest,
And for the wife who nurses
    His baby at her breast,
And for the holy maidens
    Who feed the eternal flame,
To save them from false Sextus
    That wrought the deed of shame ?

XXVIII

" Hew down the bridge, Sir Consul,
    With all the speed ye may ;
I, with two more to help me,
    Will hold the foe in play.
In yon strait path a thousand
    May well be stopped by three.
Now who will stand on either hand,
    And keep the bridge with me ? "

XXIX

Then out spake Spurius Lartius ;
    A Ramnian proud was he :
" Lo, I will stand at thy right hand,
    And keep the bridge with thee."
And out spake strong Herminius ;
    Of Titian blood was he :
" I will abide on thy left side,
    And keep the bridge with thee."

XXX

" Horatius," quoth the Consul,
    " As thou sayest, so let it be."
And straight against that great array
    Forth went the dauntless Three.

For Romans in Rome's quarrel
  Spared neither land nor gold,
Nor son nor wife, nor limb nor life,
  In the brave days of old.

XXXI

Then none was for a party;
  Then all were for the state;
Then the great man helped the poor,
  And the poor man loved the great:
Then lands were fairly portioned;
  Then spoils were fairly sold:
The Romans were like brothers
  In the brave days of old.

XXXII

Now Roman is to Roman
  More hateful than a foe,
And the Tribunes beard the high,
  And the Fathers grind the low.
As we wax hot in faction,
  In battle we wax cold:
Wherefore men fight not as they fought
  In the brave days of old.

XXXIII

Now while the Three were tightening
  Their harness on their backs,
The Consul was the foremost man
  To take in hand an axe:
And Fathers mixed with Commons,
  Seized hatchet, bar, and crow,
And smote upon the planks above,
  And loosed the props below.

XXXIV

Meanwhile the Tuscan army,
  Right glorious to behold,
Came flashing back the noonday light,
Rank behind rank, like surges bright
  Of a broad sea of gold.
Four hundred trumpets sounded
  A peal of warlike glee,
As that great host, with measured tread,
And spears advanced, and ensigns spread,
Rolled slowly towards the bridge's head,
  Where stood the dauntless Three.

XXXV

The Three stood calm and silent,
  And looked upon the foes,
And a great shout of laughter
  From all the vanguard rose:
And forth three chiefs came spurring
  Before that deep array;
To earth they sprang, their swords they drew
And lifted high their shields, and flew
  To win the narrow way;

XXXVI

Aunus from green Tifernum,
  Lord of the Hill of Vines;
And Seius, whose eight hundred slaves
  Sicken in Ilva's mines;
And Picus, long to Clusium
  Vassal in peace and war,
Who led to fight his Umbrian powers
From that gray crag where, girt with towers,
The fortress of Nequinum lowers
  O'er the pale waves of Nar.

XXXVII

Stout Lartius hurled down Aunus
    Into the stream beneath:
Herminius struck at Seius,
    And clove him to the teeth:
At Picus brave Horatius
    Darted one fiery thrust;
And the proud Umbrian's gilded arms
    Clashed in the bloody dust.

XXXVIII

Then Ocnus of Falerii
    Rushed on the Roman Three;
And Lausulus of Urgo,
    The Rover of the sea;
And Aruns of Volsinium,
    Who slew the great wild boar,
The great wild boar that had his den
Amidst the reeds of Cosa's fen,
And wasted fields, and slaughtered men,
    Along Albinia's shore.

XXXIX

Herminius smote down Aruns:
    Lartius laid Ocnus low:
Right to the heart of Lausulus
    Horatius sent a blow.
"Lie there," he cried, "fell pirate!
    No more, aghast and pale,
From Ostia's walls the crowd shall mark
The track of thy destroying bark.
No more Campania's hinds shall fly
To woods and caverns when they spy
    Thy thrice accursed sail."

XL

But now no sound of laughter
   Was heard among the foes.
A wild and wrathful clamor
   From all the vanguard rose.
Six spears' length from the entrance
   Halted that deep array,
And for a space no man came forth
   To win the narrow way.

XLI

But hark! the cry is Astur:
   And lo! the ranks divide;
And the great Lord of Luna
   Comes with his stately stride.
Upon his ample shoulders
   Clangs loud the fourfold shield,
And in his hand he shakes the brand
   Which none but he can wield.

XLII

He smiled on those bold Romans
   A smile serene and high;
He eyed the flinching Tuscans,
   And scorn was in his eye.
Quoth he, " The she-wolf's litter
   Stand savagely at bay :
But will ye dare to follow,
   If Astur clears the way?"

XLIII

Then, whirling up his broadsword
   With both hands to the height,
He rushed against Horatius,
   And smote with all his might.
With shield and blade Horatius

Right deftly turned the blow.
The blow, though turned, came yet too nigh;
It missed his helm, but gashed his thigh :
The Tuscans raised a joyful cry
   To see the red blood flow.

XLIV

He reeled, and on Herminius
   He leaned one breathing-space;
Then, like a wildcat mad with wounds,
   Sprang right at Astur's face.
Through teeth, and skull, and helmet
   So fierce a thrust he sped,
The good sword stood a hand-breadth out
   Behind the Tuscan's head.

XLV

And the great Lord of Luna
   Fell at that deadly stroke
As falls on Mount Alvernus
   A thunder-smitten oak.
Far o'er the crashing forest
   The giant arms lie spread;
And the pale augurs, muttering low,
   Gaze on the blasted head.

XLVI

On Astur's throat Horatius
   Right firmly pressed his heel,
And thrice and four times tugged amain
   Ere he wrenched out the steel.
"And see," he cried, "the welcome,
   Fair guests, that waits you here !
What noble Lucumo comes next
   To taste our Roman cheer?"

XLVII

But at this haughty challenge
    A sullen murmur ran,
Mingled of wrath, and shame, and dread,
    Along that glittering van.
There lacked not men of prowess,
    Nor men of lordly race;
For all Etruria's noblest
    Were round the fatal place.

XLVIII

But all Etruria's noblest
    Felt their hearts sink to see
On the earth the bloody corpses,
    In the path the dauntless Three:
And, from the ghastly entrance
    Where those bold Romans stood,
All shrank, like boys who unaware,
Ranging the woods to start a hare,
Come to the mouth of the dark lair
Where, growling low, a fierce old bear
    Lies amidst bones and blood.

XLIX

Was none who would be foremost
    To lead such dire attack:
But those behind cried "Forward!"
    And those before cried "Back!"
And backward now and forward
    Wavers the deep array;
And on the tossing sea of steel,
To and fro the standards reel;
And the victorious trumpet-peal
    Dies fitfully away.

L

Yet one man for one moment
　　Stood out before the crowd ;
Well known was he to all the Three,
　　And they gave him greeting loud,
" Now welcome, welcome, Sextus !
　　Now welcome to thy home !
Why dost thou stay, and turn away ?
　　Here lies the road to Rome."

LI

Thrice looked he at the city ;
　　Thrice looked he at the dead ;
And thrice came on in fury,
　　And thrice turned back in dread :
And, white with fear and hatred,
　　Scowled at the narrow way
Where, wallowing in a pool of blood,
　　The bravest Tuscans lay.

LII

But meanwhile axe and lever
　　Have manfully been plied ;
And now the bridge hangs tottering
　　Above the boiling tide.
" Come back, come back, Horatius ! "
　　Loud cried the Fathers all.
" Back, Lartius ! back, Herminius !
　　Back, ere the ruin fall ! "

LIII

Back darted Spurius Lartius ;
　　Herminius darted back :
And, as they passed, beneath their feet
　　They felt the timbers crack.

But when they turned their faces,
  And on the farther shore
Saw brave Horatius stand alone,
  They would have crossed once more.

LIV

But with a crash like thunder
  Fell every loosened beam,
And, like a dam, the mighty wreck
  Lay right athwart the stream :
And a long shout of triumph
  Rose from the walls of Rome,
As to the highest turret-tops
  Was splashed the yellow foam.

LV

And, like a horse unbroken
  When first he feels the rein,
The furious river struggled hard,
  And tossed his tawny mane,
And burst the curb, and bounded,
  Rejoicing to be free,
And whirling down, in fierce career,
Battlement, and plank, and pier,
  Rushed headlong to the sea.

LVI

Alone stood brave Horatius,
  But constant still in mind ;
Thrice thirty thousand foes before,
  And the broad flood behind.
" Down with him ! " cried false Sextus,
  With a smile on his pale face.
" Now yield thee," cried Lars Porsena,
  " Now yield thee to our grace."

LVII

Round turned he, as not deigning
   Those craven ranks to see;
Nought spake he to Lars Porsena,
   To Sextus nought spake he;
But he saw on Palatinus
   The white porch of his home;
And he spake to the noble river
   That rolls by the towers of Rome.

LVIII

"O Tiber! Father Tiber!
   To whom the Romans pray,
A Roman's life, a Roman's arms,
   Take thou in charge this day!"
So he spake, and speaking sheathed
   The good sword by his side,
And with his harness on his back,
   Plunged headlong in the tide.

LIX

No sound of joy or sorrow
   Was heard from either bank;
But friends and foes in dumb surprise,
With parted lips and straining eyes,
   Stood gazing where he sank;
And when above the surges
   They saw his crest appear,
All Rome sent forth a rapturous cry,
And even the ranks of Tuscany
   Could scarce forbear to cheer.

LX

But fiercely ran the current,
   Swollen high by months of rain:
And fast his blood was flowing;
   And he was sore in pain,

And heavy with his armor,
    And spent with changing blows:
And oft they thought him sinking,
    But still again he rose.

LXI

Never, I ween, did swimmer,
    In such an evil case,
Struggle through such a raging flood
    Safe to the landing place:
But his limbs were borne up bravely
    By the brave heart within,
And our good father Tiber
    Bore bravely up his chin.

LXII

"Curse on him!" quoth false Sextus;
    "Will not the villain drown?
But for this stay, ere close of day
    We should have sacked the town!"
"Heaven help him!" quoth Lars Porsena,
    "And bring him safe to shore;
For such a gallant feat of arms
    Was never seen before."

LXIII

And now he feels the bottom;
    Now on dry earth he stands;
Now round him throng the Fathers
    To press his gory hands;
And now, with shouts and clapping,
    And noise of weeping loud,
He enters through the River-Gate,
    Borne by the joyous crowd.

LXIV

They gave him of the corn-land,
  That was of public right,
As much as two strong oxen
  Could plough from morn till night;
And they made a molten image,
  And set it up on high,
And there it stands unto this day
  To witness if I lie.

LXV

It stands in the Comitium,
  Plain for all folk to see;
Horatius in his harness,
  Halting upon one knee:
And underneath is written,
  In letters all of gold,
How valiantly he kept the bridge
  In the brave days of old.

LXVI

And still his name sounds stirring
  Unto the men of Rome,
As the trumpet-blast that cries to them
  To charge the Volscian home;
And wives still pray to Juno
  For boys with hearts as bold
As his who kept the bridge so well
  In the brave days of old.

LXVII

And in the nights of winter,
  When the cold north winds blow,
And the long howling of the wolves
  Is heard amidst the snow;

When round the lonely cottage
  Roars loud the tempest's din,
And the good logs of Algidus
  Roar louder yet within;

LXVIII

When the oldest cask is opened,
  And the largest lamp is lit;
When the chestnuts glow in the embers,
  And the kid turns on the spit;
When young and old in circle
  Around the firebrands close;
When the girls are weaving baskets,
  And the lads are shaping bows;

LXIX

When the goodman mends his armor,
  And trims his helmet's plume;
When the goodwife's shuttle merrily
  Goes flashing through the loom;
With weeping and with laughter
  Still is the story told,
How well Horatius kept the bridge
  In the brave days of old.

The Skeleton in Armor

LONGFELLOW was always greatly interested in the legends and poetry of Northern Europe, and in this poem he tells the story of such a Viking as might well have crossed the sea with Leif, son of Eric. According to history Bjarni, the son of Herjulf, sailing west from Iceland in 986, bound for Greenland, met with dense fogs and had to steer by guesswork. After many days he came to land, but realizing it was not Greenland, he turned north and finally reached his goal. The tale of his voyage came in time to Leif, son of red Eric, and he set out in the year 1000, with thirty-five men, to find the strange land to the south. He reached the coast of Labrador, and named it "Helluland," or "slate-land." Farther south he came to densely wooded shores that he called "Markland," or "woodland," and afterwards to a country full of grapes which he christened "Vinland."

Leif and his men spent the winter in Vinland, and in the spring carried news of their discovery back to their home. But later parties of Norsemen were attacked by the native Indians when they tried to explore the new country, and in 1012 the Vikings gave up their voyages thither.

A skeleton clad in armor was discovered near Fall

River, Massachusetts, in 1835, and doubtless furnished the idea for this poem, although it was later declared to be the skeleton of an Indian, and not of a Norseman.

The lofty tower built by the Viking in the poem might have been the old stone tower which still stands at Newport, Rhode Island, and which was for a long time believed to have been built by Norsemen. Historians now claim that it was erected by Benedict Arnold, governor of Newport about 1676, who used it for a windmill. This Benedict Arnold was, of course, not the man of the same name who figured in the American Revolution.

The rhythm and flow of the poem are splendid, and the story of the young Viking who loved the blue-eyed daughter of the old Prince Hildebrand, and carried her across seas to the new Western land is as stirring as any of the hero-tales of the Scandinavian sagas.

THE SKELETON IN ARMOR

By Henry Wadsworth Longfellow

"Speak ! speak ! thou fearful guest !
    Who, with thy hollow breast
    Still in rude armor drest,
        Comest to daunt me !
    Wrapt not in Eastern balms,
    But with thy fleshless palms
    Stretched, as if asking alms,
        Why dost thou haunt me ? "

Then, from those cavernous eyes
Pale flashes seemed to rise,
As when the Northern skies
  Gleam in December;
And, like the water's flow
Under December's snow,
Came a dull voice of woe
  From the heart's chamber.

"I was a Viking old!
My deeds, though manifold,
No Skald in song has told,
  No Saga taught thee!
Take heed, that in thy verse
Thou dost the tale rehearse,
Else dread a dead man's curse;
  For this I sought thee.

"Far in the Northern Land,
By the wild Baltic's strand,
I, with my childish hand,
  Tamed the gerfalcon;
And, with my skates fast-bound,
Skimmed the half-frozen Sound,
That the poor whimpering hound
  Trembled to walk on.

"Oft to his frozen lair
Tracked I the grisly bear,
While from my path the hare
  Fled like a shadow;
Oft through the forest dark
Followed the were-wolf's bark,
Until the soaring lark
  Sang from the meadow.

"But when I older grew,
  Joining a corsair's crew,
  O'er the dark sea I flew
      With the marauders.
  Wild was the life we led;
  Many the souls that sped,
  Many the hearts that bled,
      By our stern orders.

"Many a wassail-bout
  Wore the long winter out;
  Often our midnight shout
      Set the cocks crowing.
  As we the Berserk's tale
  Measured in cups of ale,
  Draining the oaken pail,
      Filled to o'erflowing.

"Once as I told in glee
  Tales of the stormy sea,
  Soft eyes did gaze on me,
      Burning yet tender;
  And as the white stars shine
  On the dark Norway pine,
  On that dark heart of mine
      Fell their soft splendor.

"I wooed the blue-eyed maid,
  Yielding, yet half afraid,
  And in the forest's shade
      Our vows were plighted.
  Under its loosened vest
  Fluttered her little breast,
  Like birds within their nest
      By the hawk frighted.

"Bright in her father's hall
Shields gleamed upon the wall,
Loud sang the minstrels all,
    Chanting his glory;
When of old Hildebrand
I asked his daughter's hand,
Mute did the minstrels stand
    To hear my story.

"While the brown ale he quaffed,
Loud then the champion laughed,
And as the wind-gusts waft
    The sea-foam brightly,
So the loud laugh of scorn,
Out of those lips unshorn,
From the deep drinking-horn
    Blew the foam lightly.

"She was a Prince's child,
I but a Viking wild,
And though she blushed and smiled,
    I was discarded!
Should not the dove so white
Follow the sea-mew's flight,
Why did they leave that night
    Her nest unguarded?

"Scarce had I put to sea,
Bearing the maid with me,
Fairest of all was she
    Among the Norsemen!
When on the white sea-strand,
Waving his arméd hand,
Saw we old Hildebrand,
    With twenty horsemen.

" Then launched they to the blast,
Bent like a reed each mast,
Yet we were gaining fast,
    When the wind failed us ;
And with a sudden flaw
Came round the gusty Skaw,
So that our foe we saw
    Laugh as he hailed us.

" And as to catch the gale
Round veered the flapping sail,
' Death ! ' was the helmsman's hail,
    ' Death without quarter ! '
Midships with iron keel,
Struck we her ribs of steel ;
Down her black hulk did reel
    Through the black water !

" As with his wings aslant,
Sails the fierce cormorant,
Seeking some rocky haunt,
    With his prey laden,
So toward the open main,
Beating to sea again,
Through the wild hurricane,
    Bore I the maiden.

" Three weeks we westward bore,
And when the storm was o'er,
Cloudlike we saw the shore
    Stretching to leeward ;
There for my lady's bower
Built I a lofty tower,
Which, to this very hour,
    Stands looking seaward.

" There lived we many years;
   Time dried the maiden's tears;
   She had forgot her fears,
     She was a mother;
   Death closed her mild blue eyes,
   Under that tower she lies;
   Ne'er shall the sun arise
     On such another!

" Still grew my bosom then,
   Still as a stagnant fen!
   Hateful to me were men,
     The sunlight hateful!
   In the vast forest here,
   Clad in my warlike gear,
   Fell I upon my spear,
     Oh, death was grateful!

" Thus, seamed with many scars,
   Bursting these prison bars,
   Up to its native stars
     My soul ascended!
   There from the flowing bowl
   Deep drinks the warrior's soul,
   Skoal! to the Northland! *skoal!* "
     —Thus the tale ended.

IV

The Sea-King's Burial

THIS poem, written by a Scotchman, describes a strange custom of the old Norse Vikings. The kings of that northern country, when they felt that they were soon to die, had their servants lift them from bed and place them on their battle-ship. They clad the king in his armor, set his crown upon his head, and his sword in his hand. A fire was lighted in the hold of the ship. The sails were set, and the vessel headed out to sea. When the ship was far from land the flames would reach the deck, and the king would die, sword unsheathed, the winds of the ocean about him. His spirit would then go straight to the halls of Valhalla, where dwelt all the former heroes and warriors of Scandinavia.

So King Balder went out to sea in his battle-ship, and called aloud to the great All-Father, to the Norse gods Odin and Thor, and to the Vikings waiting for him.

The metre fits the story perfectly. It has the swing of the ocean waves, and the long and short lines at the end of each stanza give a strong dramatic effect. It is interesting to compare it with that other Viking poem by Longfellow, "The Skeleton in Armor."

THE SEA-KING'S BURIAL

By Charles Mackay

"My strength is failing fast,"
    Said the sea-king to his men;—
"I shall never sail the seas
    Like a conqueror again.
But while yet a drop remains
Of the life-blood in my veins,
Raise, oh, raise me from the bed;
Put the crown upon my head;
Put my good sword in my hand;
And so lead me to the strand,
Where my ship at anchor rides
        Steadily;
If I cannot end my life
In the bloody battle-strife,
Let me die as I have lived,
        On the sea."

They have raised King Balder up,
    Put his crown upon his head;
They have sheathed his limbs in mail,
    And the purple o'er him spread;
And amid the greeting rude
Of a gathering multitude,
Borne him slowly to the shore—
All the energy of yore
From his dim eyes flashing forth—
Old sea-lion of the north—
As he looked upon his ship

Riding free,
And on his forehead pale
Felt the cold refreshing gale,
And heard the welcome sound
Of the sea.

They have borne him to the ship
With a slow and solemn tread ;
They have placed him on the deck
With his crown upon his head,
Where he sat as on a throne ;
And have left him there alone,
With his anchor ready weighed,
And the snowy sails displayed
To the favoring wind, once more
Blowing freshly from the shore ;
And have bidden him farewell
Tenderly,
Saying, "King of mighty men,
We shall meet thee yet again,
In Valhalla, with the monarchs
Of the sea."

Underneath him in the hold
They have placed the lighted brand ;
And the fire was burning slow
As the vessel from the land,
Like a stag-hound from the slips,
Darted forth from out the ships.
There was music in her sail
As it swelled before the gale,
And a dashing at her prow
As it cleft the waves below,
And the good ship sped along,

Scudding free;
As on many a battle morn
In her time she had been borne,
To struggle, and to conquer
On the sea.

And the king with sudden strength
Started up, and paced the deck,
With his good sword for his staff,
And his robe around his neck:
Once alone, he raised his hand
To the people on the land;
And with shout and joyous cry
Once again they made reply,
Till the loud exulting cheer
Sounded faintly on his ear;
For the gale was o'er him blowing
Fresh and free;
And ere yet an hour had passed,
He was driven before the blast,
And a storm was on his path,
On the sea.

And still upon the deck,
While the storm about him rent,
King Balder paced about
Till his failing strength was spent.
Then he stopped awhile to rest —
Crossed his hands upon his breast,
And looked upward to the sky
With a dim but dauntless eye;
And heard the tall mast creak,
And the fitful tempest speak
Shrill and fierce, to the billows

Rushing free;
And within himself he said:
"I am coming, O ye dead!
To join you in Valhalla,
O'er the sea.

"So blow, ye tempests, blow,
And my spirit shall not quail;
I have fought with many a foe;
I have weathered many a gale;
And in this hour of death,
Ere I yield my fleeting breath —
Ere the fire now burning slow
Shall come rushing from below,
And this worn and wasted frame
Be devoted to the flame —
I will raise my voice in triumph,
Singing free;—
To the great All-Father's home
I am driving through the foam,
I am sailing to Valhalla,
O'er the sea.

"So blow, ye stormy winds —
And ye flames ascend on high;—
In the easy, idle bed
Let the slave and coward die!
But give me the driving keel,
Clang of shields and flashing steel;—
Or my foot on foreign ground,
With my enemies around!
Happy, happy, thus I'd yield,
On the deck, or in the field,
My last breath, shouting 'On

To victory.'
But since this has been denied,
They shall say that I have died
Without flinching, like a monarch
Of the sea."

And Balder spoke no more,
And no sound escaped his lip ;—
And he looked, yet scarcely saw
The destruction of his ship,
Nor the fleet sparks mounting high,
Nor the glare upon the sky ;—
Scarcely heard the billows dash,
Nor the burning timber crash ;—
Scarcely felt the scorching heat
That was gathering at his feet,
Nor the fierce flames mounting o'er him
Greedily.
But the life was in him yet,
And the courage to forget
All his pain, in his triumph
On the sea.

Once alone a cry arose,
Half of anguish, half of pride,
As he sprang upon his feet,
With the flames on every side.
"I am coming ! " said the king,
"Where the swords and bucklers ring —
Where the warrior lives again
With the souls of mighty men —
Where the weary find repose,
And the red wine ever flows ;—
I am coming, great All-Father,

Unto thee !
Unto Odin, unto Thor,
And the strong, true hearts of yore —
I am coming to Valhalla,
O'er the sea."

V

Bruce and the Spider

THIS poem tells the legendary story of how " The Bruce," Robert I, King of Scotland, after six successive defeats by the English armies, was a fugitive in a lonely hut, and there saw a spider try six times to cast his thread from one beam to another and succeed on the seventh try. Bruce took courage from the spider's perseverance, fought a seventh time, and won.

Robert Bruce was a great leader of his people, and from early youth fought against the tyranny of the English kings. The battle of Bannockburn in 1314 won freedom for Scotland and at the same time assured the crown to Bruce. Before that time he had had many rivals for the throne of Scotland, but after the battle his power over his people became so great that the parliament of the land unanimously proclaimed him king.

BRUCE AND THE SPIDER
By Bernard Barton

For Scotland's and for freedom's right
  The Bruce his part has played ; —
In five successive fields of fight
  Been conquered and dismayed :

Once more against the English host
His band he led, and once more lost
   The meed for which he fought ;
And now from battle, faint and worn,
The homeless fugitive, forlorn,
   A hut's lone shelter sought.

And cheerless was that resting-place
   For him who claimed a throne ; —
His canopy, devoid of grace,
   The rude, rough beams alone ;
The heather couch his only bed —
Yet well I ween had slumber fled
   From couch of eider down !
Through darksome night till dawn of day,
Absorbed in wakeful thought he lay
   Of Scotland and her crown.

The sun rose brightly, and its gleam
   Fell on that hapless bed,
And tinged with light each shapeless beam
   Which roofed the lowly shed ;
When, looking up with wistful eye,
The Bruce beheld a spider try
   His filmy thread to fling
From beam to beam of that rude cot —
And well the insect's toilsome lot
   Taught Scotland's future king.

Six times the gossamery thread
   The wary spider threw ; —
In vain the filmy line was sped,
   For powerless or untrue
Each aim appeared, and back recoiled
The patient insect, six times foiled,

And yet unconquered still;
And soon the Bruce, with eager eye,
Saw him prepare once more to try
   His courage, strength, and skill.

One effort more, his seventh and last ! —
   The hero hailed the sign ! —
And on the wished-for beam hung fast
   That slender silken line !
Slight as it was, his spirit caught
The more than omen ; for his thought
   The lesson well could trace,
Which even " he who runs may read,"
That Perseverance gains its meed,
   And Patience wins the race.

VI

Bannockburn

THE Scotch poet, Robert Burns, pictured to himself the national hero of Scotland, Robert Bruce, addressing his soldiers before the battle of Bannockburn, and wrote what he imagined Bruce might have said. The battle was fought near Sterling in 1314, between the Scotch and the army of Edward II of England. Bruce reminds his men of their history, of how they had bled with Wallace, a Scotch leader of the thirteenth century who had risen against the English when that people invaded the Highlands, and of how they had followed Bruce himself in many a battle. It is a fine appeal to the always ardent patriotism of his countrymen.

The English army greatly outnumbered the Scotch, but were decisively beaten, and Edward II narrowly escaped being taken prisoner.

BANNOCKBURN
By Robert Burns

At Bannockburn the English lay,—
The Scots they were na far away,
But waited for the break o' day
    That glinted in the east.

But soon the sun broke through the heath
And lighted up that field of death,
When Bruce, wi' saul-inspiring breath,
  His heralds thus addressed :—

" Scots, wha hae wi' Wallace bled —
Scots, wham Bruce has aften led —
Welcome to your gory bed,
  Or to victorie !

" Now's the day, and now's the hour ;
See the front o' battle lower ;
See approach proud Edward's power —
  Chains and slaverie !

" Wha will be a traitor knave ?
Wha can fill a coward's grave ?
Wha sae base as be a slave ?
  Let him turn and flee !

" Wha for Scotland's king and law
Freedom's sword will strongly draw,
Freeman stand or freeman fa' —
  Let him follow me !

" By oppression's woes and pains !
By your sons in servile chains !
We will drain our dearest veins,
  But they shall be free !

" Lay the proud usurpers low !
Tyrants fall in every foe !
Liberty's in every blow !
  Let us do or die ! "

VII

The Battle of Morgarten

THE Swiss people regard the battle of Morgarten as one of the noblest events in their stirring history. The small Swiss cantons, or Forest states, as they were often called, there successfully withstood the might of the powerful Austrians. It happened in this way: After the death of Henry VII, King of Germany, there was much confusion in central Europe, due to the fact that two men had been elected to succeed him, Louis of Bavaria, and Frederick the Handsome, of Austria. The Swiss canton of Schwyz began to attack the Abbey of Einsiedehn, which belonged to the Hapsburgs, of whom Frederick was the head. The Austrian ruler protested, and when he found that the rest of the Forest states sided with Schwyz, he vowed he would crush them. He gave command of his army to his brother, Duke Leopold, and the Austrians marched into Switzerland late in the autumn of 1315.

Duke Leopold divided his army, and sent one part of it, under Count Otto of Strasburg, to break into Unterwalden by the Brünig Pass. Two roads led from the town of Zug to Schwyz, and Leopold, probably through ignorance, chose the more difficult one for the troops of his own command. On November 15th he reached Ægeri, and marched along the shore of that lake, paying no attention to the enemy. He and his noblemen held the Swiss peasants in the greatest scorn, and his army was more like a hunting party than like troops ready for battle. They reached Haselmatt, and from there began to climb the steep, icy slopes of Morgarten, heading towards Schornen.

As soon as the Austrians were hemmed in by the lake and the mountains, an avalanche of boulders, rocks, and tree trunks came pouring down on the dense masses of soldiers. The Swiss peasants, few in number, knew that country well, and were posted on a mountain ridge that gave them complete command of the narrow pass of Morgarten.

While the confused Austrians tried to keep their footing the main Swiss army, from Schwyz and Uri, appeared on the other side of the pass, and rushed down upon their enemy. The Austrians were caught in a trap, and the Swiss mowed them down with their halberds, a weapon of their own invention.

In a short time the Austrian army was broken to pieces, many rushed into the lake, and those who were left fled back through the passes and out of the country. Otto of Strasburg, when he heard of the retreat of Leopold, turned back, and the forest country was soon free of all invaders.

The battle of Morgarten has sometimes been called the Swiss Thermopylæ, because a few men withstood such a great army. It was the first of a long series of great victories for the hardy mountain people, and showed them how they might maintain their independence from their vastly more powerful neighbors.

The Swiss gave thanks to God for their victory, and declared that the anniversary of the battle should be a day of thanksgiving each year.

Morgarten itself is the name given to the pasture slopes that descend to the southern end of the lake of Ægeri in the canton of Zug. A monument to the victory stands near the Haselmatt Chapel, some two miles from the station at Sattel on the railroad line from Schwyz to Zürich.

THE BATTLE OF MORGARTEN

By Felicia Dorothea Hemans

The wine-month shone in its golden prime,
　And the red grapes clustering hung,
But a deeper sound, through the Switzer's clime,
　Than the vintage-music, rung.
　　A sound, through vaulted cave,
　　A sound, through echoing glen,
　Like the hollow swell of a rushing wave;
　　— 'Twas the tread of steel-girt men.

And a trumpet, pealing wild and far,
　'Midst the ancient rocks was blown,
Till the Alps replied to that voice of war
　With a thousand of their own.
　　And through the forest-glooms
　　Flash'd helmets to the day,
　And the winds were tossing knightly plumes,
　　Like the larch-boughs in their play.

In Hasli's wilds there was gleaming steel,
 As the host of the Austrian pass'd ;
And the Schreckhorn's rocks, with a savage peal,
 Made mirth of his clarion's blast.
  Up 'midst the Righi snows
  The stormy march was heard,
 With the charger's tramp, whence fire-sparks rose,
  And the leader's gathering word.

But a band, the noblest band of all,
 Through the rude Morgarten strait,
With blazon'd streamers, and lances tall,
 Moved onwards in princely state.
  They came with heavy chains,
  For the race despised so long —
 But amidst his Alp-domains,
  The herdsman's arm is strong !

The sun was reddening the clouds of morn
 When they entered the rock defile,
And shrill as a joyous hunter's horn
 Their bugles rung the while.
  But on the misty height,
  Where the mountain-people stood,
 There was stillness, as of night,
  When storms at distance brood.

There was stillness, as of deep dead night,
 And a pause—but not of fear,
While the Switzers gazed on the gathering might
 Of the hostile shield and spear.
  On wound those columns bright
  Between the lake and wood,
 But they look'd not to the misty height
  Where the mountain-people stood.

The pass was fill'd with their serried power,
　All helm'd and mail-array'd,
And their steps had sounds like a thunder-shower
　In the rustling forest-shade.
　　There were prince and crested knight,
　　Hemm'd in by cliff and flood,
　When a shout arose from the misty height
　　Where the mountain-people stood.

And the mighty rocks came bounding down,
　Their startled foes among,
With a joyous whirl from the summit thrown —
　Oh ! the herdsman's arm is strong !
　　They came like lauwine hurl'd
　　From Alp to Alp in play,
　When the echoes shout through the snowy world
　　And the pines are borne away.

The fir-woods crash'd on the mountain-side,
　And the Switzers rush'd from high,
With a sudden charge, on the flower and pride
　Of the Austrian chivalry :
　　Like hunters of the deer,
　　They storm'd the narrow dell,
　And first in the shock, with Uri's spear,
　　Was the arm of William Tell.

There was tumult in the crowded strait,
　And a cry of wild dismay,
And many a warrior met his fate
　From a peasant's hand that day !
　　And the empire's banner then
　　From its place of waving free,
　Went down before the shepherd-men,
　　The men of the Forest-sea.

With their pikes and massy clubs they brake
　The cuirass and the shield,
And the war-horse dash'd to the reddening lake
　From the reapers of the field !
　　The field—but not of sheaves —
　　Proud crests and pennons lay,
　　Strewn o'er it thick as the birch-wood leaves,
　　In the autumn tempest's way.

Oh ! the sun in heaven fierce havoc view'd,
　When the Austrian turn'd to fly,
And the brave, in the trampling multitude,
　Had a fearful death to die !
　　And the leader of the war
　　At eve unhelm'd was seen,
　　With a hurrying step on the wilds afar,
　　And a pale and troubled mien.

But the sons of the land which the freeman tills,
　Went back from the battle-toil,
To their cabin homes 'midst the deep green hills,
　All burden'd with royal spoil.
　　There were songs and festal fires
　　On the soaring Alps that night,
　　When children sprung to greet their sires
　　From the wild Morgarten fight.

VIII

Chevy-Chase

THIS is a very old English ballad, and the author of it is unknown. The title actually means the hunt or chase among the Cheviot Hills which divide England and Scotland. According to the story there had long been keen rivalry between the families of Percy, Earl of Northumberland in England, and of the Scotch Earl of Douglas. Each made continual raids into the other's territory. One day Earl Percy vowed that he would hunt for three days in the Scotch border, or Cheviot Hills, without asking leave of the Douglas. He set out to do this, but as soon as the hunt begins the ballad mixes with it an account of the Battle of Otterburn, which was fought by English and Scotch in 1388 in the county of Northumberland, and which resulted in a Scotch victory.

The poem describes both the hunt and the battle, but many of the facts are incorrectly given. Earl Percy's son, Henry, known as Hotspur, killed Earl Douglas at Otterburn, although here Douglas is described as being killed by the arrow of an English archer. The English king is called Henry, and the Scotch James, but in 1388 Richard II was king of England, and Robert II king of Scotland. In return for the English defeat at Otterburn, they did, as the

CHEVY CHASE

Sir Edwin Landseer

poem states, win a great victory over the Scotch at
Humbledown in Northumberland in 1402.

Many of these old ballads contain curious mixtures
of several poems, made into one years after the events
described. This is a very good example of such a
combination, and one of the best of the old popular
narratives in rhyme.

CHEVY-CHASE

Anonymous

God prosper long our noble king,
　　Our lives and safeties all ;
A woful hunting once there did
　　In Chevy-Chase befall.

To drive the deer with hound and horn
　　Earl Percy took his way ;
The child may rue that is unborn
　　The hunting of that day.

The stout earl of Northumberland
　　A vow to God did make,
His pleasure in the Scottish woods
　　Three summer days to take —

The chiefest harts in Chevy-Chase
　　To kill and bear away.
These tidings to Earl Douglas came,
　　In Scotland where he lay ;

Who sent Earl Percy present word
　　He would prevent his sport.
The English earl, not fearing that,
　　Did to the woods resort.

With fifteen hundred bowmen bold,
  All chosen men of might,
Who knew full well in time of need
  To aim their shafts aright.

The gallant greyhounds swiftly ran
  To chase the fallow deer;
On Monday they began to hunt
  When daylight did appear;

And long before high noon they had
  A hundred fat bucks slain;
Then having dined, the drovers went
  To rouse the deer again.

The bowmen mustered on the hills,
  Well able to endure;
And all their rear, with special care,
  That day was guarded sure.

The hounds ran swiftly through the woods,
  The nimble deer to take,
That with their cries the hills and dales
  An echo shrill did make.

Lord Percy to the quarry went,
  To view the slaughtered deer;
Quoth he, "Earl Douglas promised
  This day to meet me here;

"But if I thought he would not come,
  No longer would I stay;"
With that a brave young gentleman
  Thus to the earl did say:

" Lo, yonder doth Earl Douglas come,
　　His men in armor bright ;
　Full twenty hundred Scottish spears
　　All marching in our sight ;

" All men of pleasant Teviotdale,
　　Fast by the river Tweed ; "
" Then cease your sports," Earl Percy said,
　　" And take your bows with speed ;

" And now with me, my countrymen,
　　Your courage forth advance ;
　For never was there champion yet,
　　In Scotland or in France,

" That ever did on horseback come,
　　But if my hap it were,
　I durst encounter man for man,
　　With him to break a spear."

Earl Douglas on his milk-white steed,
　　Most like a baron bold,
Rode foremost of his company,
　　Whose armor shone like gold.

" Show me," said he, " whose men you be,
　　That hunt so boldly here,
That, without my consent, do chase
　　And kill my fallow-deer."

The first man that did answer make,
　　Was noble Percy he—
Who said, " We list not to declare,
　　Nor show whose men we be :

"Yet will we spend our dearest blood
    Thy chiefest harts to slay."
Then Douglas swore a solemn oath,
    And thus in rage did say:

"Ere thus I will out-braved be,
    One of us two shall die;
I know thee well, an earl thou art —
    Lord Percy, so am I.

"But trust me, Percy, pity it were,
    And great offence, to kill
Any of these our guiltless men,
    For they have done no ill.

"Let you and me the battle try,
    And set our men aside."
"Accursed be he," Earl Percy said,
    "By whom this is denied."

Then stepped a gallant squire forth,
    Witherington was his name,
Who said, "I would not have it told
    To Henry, our king, for shame,

"That e'er my captain fought on foot,
    And I stood looking on.
You two be earls," said Witherington,
    "And I a squire alone;

"I'll do the best that do I may,
    While I have power to stand;
While I have power to wield my sword,
    I'll fight with heart and hand."

Our English archers bent their bows —
   Their hearts were good and true ;
At the first flight of arrows sent,
   Full fourscore Scots they slew.

Yet stays Earl Douglas on the bent,
   As chieftain stout and good ;
As valiant captain, all unmoved,
   The shock he firmly stood.

His host he parted had in three,
   As leader ware and tried ;
And soon his spearmen on their foes
   Bore down on every side.

Throughout the English archery
   They dealt full many a wound ;
But still our valiant Englishmen
   All firmly kept their ground.

And throwing straight their bows away,
   They grasped their swords so bright ;
And now sharp blows, a heavy shower,
   On shields and helmets light.

They closed full fast on every side —
   No slackness there was found ;
And many a gallant gentleman
   Lay gasping on the ground.

In truth, it was a grief to see
   How each one chose his spear,
And how the blood out of their breasts
   Did gush like water clear.

At last these two stout earls did meet;
  Like captains of great might,
Like lions wode, they laid on lode,
  And made a cruel fight.

They fought until they both did sweat,
  With swords of tempered steel,
Until the blood, like drops of rain,
  They trickling down did feel.

"Yield thee, Lord Percy," Douglas said;
  "In faith I will thee bring
Where thou shalt high advanced be
  By James, our Scottish king.

"Thy ransom I will freely give,
  And this report of thee,
Thou art the most courageous knight
  That ever I did see."

"No, Douglas," saith Earl Percy then,
  "Thy proffer I do scorn;
I will not yield to any Scot
  That ever yet was born."

With that there came an arrow keen
  Out of an English bow,
Which struck Earl Douglas to the heart,
  A deep and deadly blow;

Who never spake more words than these:
  "Fight on, my merry men all;
For why, my life is at an end;
  Lord Percy sees my fall."

Then leaving life, Earl Percy took
 The dead man by the hand ;
And said, " Earl Douglas, for thy life
 Would I had lost my land.

" In truth, my very heart doth bleed
 With sorrow for thy sake ;
For sure a more redoubted knight
 Mischance did never take."

A knight amongst the Scots there was
 Who saw Earl Douglas die,
Who straight in wrath did vow revenge
 Upon the Earl Percy.

Sir Hugh Mountgomery was he called,
 Who, with a spear full bright,
Well mounted on a gallant steed,
 Ran fiercely through the fight ;

And past the English archers all,
 Without a dread or fear ;
And through Earl Percy's body then
 He thrust his hateful spear ;

With such vehement force and might
 He did his body gore,
The staff ran through the other side
 A large cloth-yard and more.

So thus did both these nobles die,
 Whose courage none could stain.
An English archer then perceived
 The noble earl was slain.

He had a bow bent in his hand,
 Made of a trusty tree;
An arrow of a cloth-yard long
 To the hard head haled he.

Against Sir Hugh Mountgomery
 So right the shaft he set,
The gray goose wing that was thereon
 In his heart's blood was wet.

This fight did last from break of day
 Till setting of the sun :
For when they rung the evening-bell,
 The battle scarce was done.

With stout Earl Percy there were slain
 Sir John of Egerton,
Sir Robert Ratcliff, and Sir John,
 Sir James, that bold baron.

And with Sir George and stout Sir James,
 Both knights of good account,
Good Sir Ralph Raby there was slain,
 Whose prowess did surmount.

For Witherington my heart is wo
 That ever he slain should be,
For when his legs were hewn in two,
 He knelt and fought on his knee.

And with Earl Douglas there was slain
 Sir Hugh Mountgomery,
Sir Charles Murray, that from the field
 One foot would never flee.

Sir Charles Murray of Ratcliff, too-
   His sister's son was he;
Sir David Lamb, so well esteemed,
   But saved he could not be.

And the Lord Maxwell in like case
   Did with Earl Douglas die:
Of twenty hundred Scottish spears,
   Scarce fifty-five did fly.

Of fifteen hundred Englishmen,
   Went home but fifty-three;
The rest in Chevy-Chase were slain,
   Under the greenwood tree.

Next day did many widows come,
   Their husbands to bewail;
They washed their wounds in brinish tears,
   But all would not prevail.

Their bodies, bathed in purple blood,
   They bore with them away;
They kissed them dead a thousand times,
   Ere they were clad in clay.

The news was brought to Edinburgh,
   Where Scotland's king did reign,
That brave Earl Douglas suddenly
   Was with an arrow slain:

' Oh, heavy news," King James did say;
   " Scotland can witness be
I have not any captain more
   Of such account as he."

Like tidings to King Henry came
    Within as short a space,
That Percy of Northumberland
    Was slain in Chevy-Chase:

" Now God be with him," said our king,
    " Since 'twill no better be;
I trust I have within my realm
    Five hundred as good as he:

" Yet shall not Scots or Scotland say
    But I will vengeance take:
I'll be revenged on them all,
    For brave Earl Percy's sake."

This vow full well the king performed
    After at Humbledown;
In one day fifty knights were slain,
    With lords of high renown;

And of the best, of small account,
    Did many hundreds die:
Thus endeth the hunting of Chevy-Chase,
    Made by the Earl Percy.

God save the king, and bless this land,
    With plenty, joy, and peace;
And grant, henceforth, that foul debate
    'Twixt noblemen may cease!

IX

Ivry

THIS splendid poem tells of the battle of Ivry, fought
in 1590 between the Huguenots, or Protestants, under
Henry of Navarre, and the Catholics, led by the Duke
of Mayenne. Navarre was a small kingdom lying
partly in France and partly in Spain, and Henry's
mother was its queen. The king of France, Henry III,
had tried to reconcile the Catholics and Huguenots, but
the Catholics distrusted him, and formed a "League"
to fight for their faith. This brought about a great
civil war in France.

Henry III was assassinated in 1589. He had chosen
his cousin, Henry of Navarre, to succeed him, but the
leaders of the League and the people of Paris opposed
this. Henry of Navarre defeated Mayenne at Ivry,
which is about thirty miles west of Paris, and as a result
of this victory became undisputed king of France. He
made a wise ruler, and was one of the best loved of all
French kings. He was famous for his gallant bearing,
his chivalry, and his bravery, all of which he had shown
very strikingly at Ivry.

Macaulay pictures the enthusiasm of a follower of
Henry at the battle. The Huguenots have won, thanks
to the Lord of Hosts and their king, and there shall be

rejoicing in the city of La Rochelle, a Huguenot strong-hold on the western coast of France.

Then the Huguenot soldier describes the battle. The army of the Catholic League faced them, made up of citizens led by priests and rebellious nobles, Swiss infantry under Appenzel, spearmen brought from Flanders by Philip, Count of Egmont, the troopers of the Guise family, who came from the province of Lorraine, with the Duke of Mayenne him-self in command of them. As the Huguenots looked at their enemies they remembered the Massacre of St. Bartholomew in 1572, when Catherine de' Medici had tried to kill all the Huguenots in France, and had killed so many in Paris that the River Seine ran with blood; and they remembered that their great leader, Admiral Coligny, had been one of the first to fall.

Then Henry of Navarre rode out before his troops, with a snow-white plume fastened to his helmet. He bade his men follow him, and if the standard-bearer fell to take his white plume for their guide and flag of battle.

The enemy charged, the Duke of Mayenne leading the mercenary troops of Guelders and Almayne across the open field. A thousand Huguenot knights set their spears in rest, and followed Henry's plume as he dashed forward. The armies met, and Mayenne was driven back, the Duke d'Aumale forced to surrender, and the Count of Egmont killed. The Huguenots raised the cry, " Remember St. Bartholomew ! " but Henry called to them to pursue the foreign soldiers' but to spare their French brothers. As if to mark the

IVRY

downfall of the great Catholic house of Guise, the Huguenot Duke of Sully, Baron of Rosny, captured the black and white standard of that family.

The poem ends with a call to the daughters and wives of Vienna and Lucerne to weep for their fathers and husbands who had been killed fighting for the League, to Philip II of Spain, an ally of Mayenne, to send his Mexican gold to Antwerp so that the monks might pray for his Flemish spearmen, to the soldiers of the League to be prepared for further battle, and to the people of St. Geneviève's city of Paris to watch for the victorious arrival of the Huguenots under their valiant king.

In this poem Macaulay catches the gallant spirit of the follower of Henry of Navarre as vividly as he describes the simple patriotism of a citizen of the Roman Republic in " Horatius."

IVRY

By Thomas Babbington, Lord Macaulay

Now glory to the Lord of Hosts, from whom all glories are !
And glory to our Sovereign Liege, King Henry of Navarre !
Now let there be the merry sound of music and of dance,
Through thy corn-fields green, and sunny vines, O pleasant land
    of France !
And thou, Rochelle, our own Rochelle, proud city of the waters,
Again let rapture light the eyes of all thy mourning daughters.
As thou wert constant in our ills, be joyous in our joy,
For cold, and stiff, and still are they who wrought thy walls annoy.
Hurrah ! Hurrah ! a single field hath turned the chance of war,
Hurrah ! Hurrah ! for Ivry, and Henry of Navarre.

Oh ! how our hearts were beating, when at the dawn of day
We saw the army of the League drawn out in long array ;
With all its priest-led citizens, and all its rebel peers,
And Appenzel's stout infantry, and Egmont's Flemish spears.
There rode the brood of false Lorraine, the curses of our land ;
And dark Mayenne was in the midst, a truncheon in his hand :
And, as we looked on them, we thought of Seine's empurpled flood,
And good Coligni's hoary hair all dabbled with his blood ;
And we cried unto the living God, who rules the fate of war,
To fight for His own holy name, and Henry of Navarre.

The King is come to marshal us, in all his armor drest,
And he has bound a snow-white plume upon his gallant crest.
He looked upon his people, and a tear was in his eye ;
He looked upon the traitors, and his glance was stern and high.
Right graciously he smiled on us, as rolled from wing to wing,
Down all our line, a deafening shout, "God save our Lord the
    King ! "
" And if my standard-bearer fall, as fall full well he may,
For never saw I promise yet of such a bloody fray,
Press where ye see my white plume shine, amidst the ranks of
    war,
And be your oriflamme to-day the helmet of Navarre."

Hurrah ! the foes are moving.   Hark to the mingled din
Of fife, and steed, and trump, and drum, and roaring culverin.
The fiery Duke is pricking fast across Saint André's plain,
With all the hireling chivalry of Guelders and Almayne.
Now by the lips of those ye love, fair gentlemen of France,
Charge for the golden lilies,—upon them with the lance.
A thousand spurs are striking deep, a thousand spears in rest,
A thousand knights are pressing close behind the snow-white
    crest ;
And in they burst, and on they rushed, while, like a guiding star,
Amidst the thickest carnage blazed the helmet of Navarre.

Now, God be praised, the day is ours.   Mayenne hath turned his
     rein.
D'Aumale hath cried for quarter.   The Flemish count is slain.
Their ranks are breaking like thin clouds before a Biscay gale;
The field is heaped with bleeding steeds, and flags, and cloven
     mail.
And then we thought on vengeance, and, all along our van,
"Remember St. Bartholomew," was passed from man to man.
But out spake gentle Henry, "No Frenchman is my foe:
Down, down with every foreigner, but let your brethren go."
Oh ! was there ever such a knight, in friendship or in war,
As our Sovereign Lord, King Henry, the soldier of Navarre ?

Right well fought all the Frenchmen who fought for France to-
     day;
And many a lordly banner God gave them for a prey.
But we of the religion have borne us best in fight ;
And the good Lord of Rosny hath ta'en the cornet white.
Our own true Maximilian the cornet white hath ta'en,
The cornet white with crosses black, the flag of false Lorraine.
Up with it high; unfurl it wide; that all the host may know
How God hath humbled the proud house which wrought His
     church such woe.
Then on the ground, while trumpets sound their loudest point of
     war,
Fling the red shreds, a footcloth neat for Henry of Navarre.

Ho ! maidens of Vienna ; ho ! matrons of Lucerne ;
Weep, weep, and rend your hair for those who never shall return.
Ho ! Philip, send, for charity, thy Mexican pistoles,
That Antwerp monks may sing a mass for thy poor spearmen's
     souls.
Ho ! gallant nobles of the League, look that your arms be bright;
Ho ! burghers of Saint Geneviève, keep watch and ward to-night.

For our God hath crushed the tyrant, our God hath raised the
slave,
And mocked the counsel of the wise, and the valor of the brave.
Then glory to His holy name, from whom all glories are ;
And glory to our Sovereign Lord, King Henry of Navarre.

X

The *Revenge*

THIS ballad of the *Revenge* tells a true story of the war that was fought between Queen Elizabeth of England and Philip II of Spain. A fleet of six English ships was overtaken at the Azore Islands in August, 1591, by fifty-three Spanish men-of-war, many of them of very large size and carrying big guns. The English ships were in need of repairs, and many of their sailors were ill on shore. The Admiral, Lord Thomas Howard, seeing how great were the odds against him, gave orders to fly at once. But Sir Richard Grenville, commander of the small ship *Revenge*, said that more than ninety of his crew were ill on shore, and that he could not leave them there to fall into the hands of the Spaniards, who would treat them as heretics and ill-use them.

The Admiral left with his five ships, and Sir Richard carried all his sick sailors, men from Bideford in Devonshire, on board the *Revenge*, while they blessed him for not surrendering them to the cruel Spaniards. Then he sailed from the Azores, with a crew of only a hundred men.

The Spanish fleet, built so high at bow and stern that they looked like castles on the water, caught up with the *Revenge*. Sir Richard sent his little craft straight through the enemy's men-of-war, and fought them all that afternoon and all that night. At dawn they were still fighting, and then Sir Richard wanted to sink his ship rather than let her fall into the hands of Spain. But his men protested, saying they could get honorable terms of surrender from their foes.

Sir Richard was wounded and dying when his men yielded. The Spaniards carried him like a hero to their flag-ship, where he died. Then they manned the little *Revenge* with their own crew, and the whole fleet set sail. But that night a great gale rose and shattered the Spanish fleet, and together with the other ships the *Revenge* sank at sea.

Tennyson follows the account of the actual sea-fight closely. The words of Sir Richard as he fell on the deck of the Spanish man-of-war are said to have been: "Here die I, Richard Grenville, with a joyful and quiet mind; for I have ended my life as a good soldier ought to do, who has fought for his country and his queen, for his honor and religion."

THE *REVENGE*

By *Alfred, Lord Tennyson*

(A Ballad of the Fleet)
(August, 1591)

At Flores in the Azores, Sir Richard Grenville lay,
And a pinnace, like a fluttered bird, came flying from far away:
"Spanish ships-of-war at sea! we have sighted fifty-three!"
Then sware Lord Thomas Howard: "'Fore God I am no coward;
But I cannot meet them here, for my ships are out of gear,
And the half my men are sick. I must fly but follow quick.

We are six ships of the line; can we fight with fifty-three?"
Then spake Sir Richard Grenville: "I know you are no coward;
You fly them for a moment to fight with them again.
But I've ninety men and more that are lying sick ashore.
I should count myself the coward if I left them, my Lord Howard,
To these Inquisition dogs and the devildoms of Spain."

So Lord Howard passed away with five ships-of-war that day,
Till he melted like a cloud in the silent summer heaven;
But Sir Richard bore in hand all his sick men from the land
Very carefully and slow,
Men of Bideford in Devon,
And we laid them on the ballast down below;
For we brought them all aboard,
And they blest him in their pain, that they were not left to Spain,
To the thumbscrew and the stake, for the glory of the Lord.

He had only a hundred seamen to work the ship and to fight,
And he sailed away from Flores till the Spaniard came in sight,
With his huge sea-castles heaving upon the weather-bow.
"Shall we fight or shall we fly?
Good Sir Richard, tell us now,
For to fight is but to die!
There'll be little of us left by the time this sun be set."
And Sir Richard said again: "We be all good Englishmen.
Let us bang these dogs of Seville, the children of the devil,
For I never turned my back upon don or devil yet."

Sir Richard spoke and he laughed, and we roared a hurrah, and so
The little *Revenge* ran on sheer into the heart of the foe,
With her hundred fighters on deck, and her ninety sick below;
For half of their fleet to the right and half to the left were seen,
And the little *Revenge* ran on through the long sea-lane between.

Thousands of their soldiers looked down from their decks and
    laughed,
Thousands of their seamen made mock at the mad little craft
Running on and on, till delayed
By their mountain-like *San Philip* that, of fifteen hundred tons,
And up-shadowing high above us with her yawning tiers of guns,
Took the breath from our sails, and we stayed.

And while now the great *San Philip* hung above us like a cloud,
Whence the thunderbolt will fall
Long and loud,
Four galleons drew away
From the Spanish fleet that day,
And two upon the larboard and two upon the starboard lay,
And the battle-thunder broke from them all.

But anon the great *San Philip*, she bethought herself and went,
Having that within her womb that had left her ill-content;
And the rest they came aboard us, and they fought us hand to
    hand,
For a dozen times they came with their pikes and musqueteers,
And a dozen times we shook 'em off as a dog that shakes his ears,
When he leaps from the water to the land.

And the sun went down, and the stars came out far over the
    summer sea,
But never a moment ceased the fight of the one and the fifty-three.
Ship after ship, the whole night long, their high-built galleons came,
Ship after ship, the whole night long, with her battle-thunder and
    flame;
Ship after ship, the whole night long, drew back with her dead
    and her shame.
For some were sunk and many were shattered, and so could fight
    us no more —
God of battles, was ever a battle like this in the world before?

For he said, "Fight on ! fight on ! "
Though his vessel was all but a wreck ;
And it chanced that, when half of the summer night was gone,
With a grisly wound to be drest, he had left the deck,
But a bullet struck him that was dressing it suddenly dead,
And himself, he was wounded again in the side and the head.
And he said, "Fight on ! fight on ! "

And the night went down, and the sun smiled out far over the
    summer sea,
And the Spanish fleet with broken sides lay round us all in a ring ;
But they dared not touch us again, for they feared that we still
    could sting,
So they watched what the end would be.
And we had not fought them in vain,
But in perilous plight were we,
Seeing forty of our poor hundred were slain,
And half of the rest of us maimed for life
In the crash of the cannonades and the desperate strife ;
And the sick men down in the hold were most of them stark and
    cold,
And the pikes were all broken or bent, and the powder was all of
    it spent ;
And the masts and the rigging were lying over the side ;

But Sir Richard cried in his English pride,
"We have fought such a fight, for a day and a night,
As may never be fought again !
We have won great glory, my men !
And a day less or more
At sea or ashore,
We die—does it matter when ?
Sink me the ship, Master Gunner—sink her, split her in twain !
Fall into the hands of God, not into the hands of Spain ! "

And the gunner said " Ay, ay," but the seamen made reply:
" We have children, we have wives,
And the Lord hath spared our lives.
We will make the Spaniard promise, if we yield, to let us go ;
We shall live to fight again and to strike another blow."
And the lion there lay dying, and they yielded to the foe.

And the stately Spanish men to their flag-ship bore him then,
Where they laid him by the mast, old Sir Richard caught at last,
And they praised him to his face with their courtly foreign grace ;
But he rose upon their decks, and he cried :
" I have fought for Queen and Faith like a valiant man and true ;
I have only done my duty as a man is bound to do :
With a joyful spirit I, Sir Richard Grenville, die ! "
And he fell upon their decks, and he died.

And they stared at the dead that had been so valiant and true,
And had holden the power and glory of Spain so cheap
That he dared her with one little ship and his English few ;
Was he devil or man ?   He was devil for aught they knew,
But they sank his body with honor down into the deep,
And they manned the *Revenge* with a swarthier, alien crew,
And away she sailed with her loss and longed for her own ;

When a wind from the lands they had ruined awoke from sleep,
And the water began to heave and the weather to moan,
And or ever that evening ended, a great gale blew,
And a wave like the wave that is raised by an earthquake grew,
Till it smote on their hulls and their sails and their masts and
    their flags,
And the whole sea plunged and fell on the shot-shattered navy of
    Spain,
And the little *Revenge* herself went down by the island crags,
To be lost evermore in the main.

XI

A Legend of Bregenz

THIS is a story of the old city of Bregenz that stands on the shore of Lake Constance, on the borders of Switzerland, Germany, and that province of Austria called the Tyrol. A girl of Bregenz left her home and went to a Swiss village to live. She entered a household there, taught her master's children, and tended his cattle. The people were kind to her, and in time she forgot that she was among strangers. But one day she learned that the Swiss were planning to attack Bregenz by stealth. Instantly all her old love of home awoke. She stole from the house at night, mounted a horse, and rode to Bregenz, hoping to warn the city before the Swiss soldiers should arrive. She had to cross the Rhine, but her steed carried her safely over, and she reached Bregenz in time.

The brave girl became the greatest heroine of her city; a picture of her on her charger is carved over the stone gateway on the hill, and the watchman of Bregenz calls her name each midnight.

A LEGEND OF BREGENZ
By Adelaide A. Procter

Girt round with rugged mountains the fair Lake Constance lies;
In her blue heart reflected, shine back the starry skies;
And, watching each white cloudlet float silently and slow,
You think a piece of heaven lies on our earth below!

Midnight is there; and silence, enthroned in heaven, looks down
Upon her own calm mirror, upon a sleeping town :
For Bregenz, that quaint city upon the Tyrol shore,
Has stood above Lake Constance a thousand years and more.

Her battlements and towers, upon their rocky steep,
Have cast their trembling shadows for ages on the deep ;
Mountain and lake and valley, a sacred legend know,
Of how the town was saved one night, three hundred years ago.

Far from her home and kindred a Tyrol maid had fled,
To serve in the Swiss valleys, and toil for daily bread ;
And every year that fleeted so silently and fast
Seem'd to bear further from her the memory of the past.

She served kind, gentle masters, nor ask'd for rest or change ;
Her friends seem'd no more new ones, their speech seem'd no
    more strange ;
And, when she led her cattle to pasture every day,
She ceased to look and wonder on which side Bregenz lay.

She spoke no more of Bregenz, with longing and with tears ;
Her Tyrol home seem'd faded in a deep mist of years ;
She heeded not the rumors of Austrian war or strife ;
Each day she rose, contented, to the calm toils of life.

Yet, when her master's children would clustering round her stand,
She sang them the old ballads of her own native land ;
And, when at morn and evening she knelt before God's throne,
The accents of her childhood rose to her lips alone.

And so she dwelt : the valley more peaceful year by year ;
When suddenly strange portents of some great deed seem'd near.
The golden corn was bending upon its fragile stalk,
While farmers, heedless of their fields, paced up and down in
    talk.

The men seem'd stern and alter'd, with looks cast on the ground;
With anxious faces, one by one, the women gather'd round;
All talk of flax, or spinning, or work, was put away;
The very children seem'd afraid to go alone to play.

One day, out in the meadow with strangers from the town,
Some secret plan discussing, the men walk'd up and down.
Yet now and then seem'd watching a strange, uncertain gleam,
That look'd like lances 'mid the trees that stood below the stream.

At eve they all assembled, all care and doubt were fled;
With jovial laugh they feasted, the board was nobly spread.
The elder of the village rose up, his glass in hand,
And cried, " We drink the downfall of an accursed land !

" The night is growing darker; ere one more day is flown
Bregenz, our foeman's stronghold, Bregenz shall be our own ! "
The women shrank in terror, (yet pride, too, had her part,)
But one poor Tyrol maiden felt death within her heart.

Before her stood fair Bregenz, once more her towers arose;
What were the friends beside her ?   Only her country's foes !
The faces of her kinsfolk, the days of childhood flown,
The echoes of her mountains, reclaim'd her as their own !

Nothing she heard around her, (though shouts rang forth again,)
Gone were the green Swiss valleys, the pasture, and the plain;
Before her eyes one vision, and in her heart one cry,
That said, " Go forth, save Bregenz, and then, if need be, die ! "

With trembling haste and breathless, with noiseless step she sped;
Horses and weary cattle were standing in the shed;
She loosed the strong white charger, that fed from out her hand,
She mounted and she turn'd his head towards her native land.

Out—out into the darkness—faster, and still more fast;
The smooth grass flies behind her, the chestnut wood is pass'd;
She looks up; clouds are heavy: Why is her steed so slow? —
Scarcely the wind beside them can pass them as they go.

"Faster!" she cries, "O, faster!" Eleven the church-bells
    chime:
"O God," she cries, "help Bregenz, and bring me there in
    time!"
But louder than bells' ringing, or lowing of the kine,
Grows nearer in the midnight the rushing of the Rhine.

Shall not the roaring waters their headlong gallop check?
The steed draws back in terror, she leans above his neck
To watch the flowing darkness, the bank is high and steep;
One pause,—he staggers forward, and plunges in the deep.

She strives to pierce the blackness, and looser throws the rein;
Her steed must breast the waters that dash above his mane;
How gallantly, how nobly, he struggles through the foam,
And see, in the far distance shine out the lights of home!

Up the steep bank he bears her, and now they rush again
Toward the heights of Bregenz, that tower above the plain.
They reach the gate of Bregenz just as the midnight rings,
And out come serf and soldier to meet the news she brings.

Bregenz is saved! Ere daylight her battlements are mann'd;
Defiance greets the army that marches on the land:
And, if to deeds heroic should endless fame be paid,
Bregenz does well to honor the noble Tyrol maid.

Three hundred years are vanish'd, and yet upon the hill
An old stone gateway rises, to do her honor still.
And there, when Bregenz women sit spinning in the shade,
They see in quaint old carving the charger and the maid.

And when, to guard old Bregenz, by gateway, street, and tower,
The warder paces all night long, and calls each passing hour:
" Nine," " ten," " eleven," he cries aloud, and then (O crown
    of fame !)
When midnight pauses in the skies he calls the maiden's name.

XII

Landing of the Pilgrim Fathers

A LITTLE band of English men and women, who had left their homes because of religious persecution, sailed from Southampton, in England, on August 15, 1620. They had two vessels, the *Mayflower* and the *Speedwell*. The *Speedwell* soon proved unseaworthy and had to put back to Plymouth for repairs, while twelve of her thirty voyagers were added to the ninety who were already on board the *Mayflower*.

Nine weeks later land was sighted, and on the evening of November 19, 1620, the pilgrims brought their ship into what came to be known as Cape Cod harbor. Two days later the *Mayflower* dropped anchor off what is now Provincetown, which is the extreme point of Cape Cod, and a band of sixteen men, headed by Captain Miles Standish, landed to explore the shore. The first actual settlement was made a month later, on December 21, 1620, at Plymouth, a more protected harbor than that of Provincetown.

This desire of the Pilgrims for a place where they might be free to worship God as they pleased was the cause of the founding of the first colony in New England.

The Landing of the Pilgrims

LANDING OF THE PILGRIM FATHERS
By Felicia Dorothea Hemans

The breaking waves dashed high
  On a stern and rock-bound coast,
And the woods against a stormy sky
  Their giant branches tossed ;

And the heavy night hung dark,
  The hills and waters o'er,
When a band of exiles moored their bark
  On the wild New England shore.

Not as the conqueror comes,
  They, the true-hearted, came ;
Not with the roll of the stirring drums,
  And the trumpet that sings of fame ;

Not as the flying come,
  In silence and in fear ;
They shook the depths of the desert gloom
  With their hymns of lofty cheer.

Amidst the storm they sang,
  And the stars heard, and the sea ;
And the sounding aisles of the dim woods rang
  To the anthem of the free.

The ocean eagle soared
  From his nest by the white wave's foam ;
And the rocking pines of the forest roared —
  This was their welcome home.

There were men with hoary hair
  Amidst that pilgrim band :
Why had they come to wither there,
  Away from their childhood's land ?

There was woman's fearless eye,
  Lit by her deep love's truth ;
There was manhood's brow, serenely high,
  And the fiery heart of youth.

What sought they thus afar ?
  Bright jewels of the mine ?
The wealth of seas, the spoils of war ?
  They sought a faith's pure shrine !

Ay, call it holy ground,
  The soil where first they trod ;
They have left unstained what there they found —
  Freedom to worship God.

XIII

The Cavalier's Escape

THE Civil War in England was fought during the years from 1642 to 1649 between the followers of King Charles I, who were called the "Cavaliers," and the men led by Oliver Cromwell, who sided with the Parliament, and were called "Roundheads," because they wore their hair cut short. In this poem one of the Cavaliers has met a band of Roundheads, and is trying to outride them and reach his own men at the town of Salisbury, five miles away. His chestnut mare Kate can outstrip both the roan and the gray that are following her.

It is almost dawn as the Cavalier starts. He hears the heavy hoof-beats of the roan, and the quicker tread of the gray. But Kate dashes off ahead of them, and her rider doffs his hat in mock courtesy and wishes his pursuers good-day. They splash through the mire and come to a gate. Kate clears it, but the others falter. The Cavalier gains a lead, but soon the Roundheads are close behind him again. He turns like a stag at bay, strikes a blow at the first pursuer and drops him from his horse; the second fires, but misses, and the Cavalier wounds him with a stroke of his sword. Then he fights his way through the others who have caught up, and dashes on. The enemy follow with sword and match-lock gun. They are almost on him when he reaches Salisbury gate. One long leap by the faithful chestnut steed, and he is safe within the town, leaving the Roundheads baffled of their prey.

The Cavalier calls them the "canting band" because the Roundheads were supposed to be religious zealots, and fond of cant and hypocrisy from the standpoint of the dashing Cavaliers.

THE CAVALIER'S ESCAPE
By Walter Thornbury

Trample ! trample ! went the roan,
    Trap ! trap! went the gray ;
But pad ! *pad !* PAD ! like a thing that was mad,
    My chestnut broke away.
It was just five miles from Salisbury town,
    And but one hour to day.

Thud ! THUD ! came on the heavy roan,
    Rap ! RAP ! the mettled gray ;
But my chestnut mare was of blood so rare,
    That she showed them all the way.
Spur on ! spur on !—I doffed my hat,
    And wished them all good-day.

They splashed through miry rut and pool,—
    Splintered through fence and rail ;
But chestnut Kate switched over the gate,—
    I saw them droop and tail.
To Salisbury town—but a mile of down,
    Once over this brook and rail.

Trap! trap! I heard their echoing hoofs
 Past the walls of mossy stone;
The roan flew on at a staggering pace,
 But blood is better than bone.
I patted old Kate, and gave her the spur,
 For I knew it was all my own.

But trample! trample! came their steeds,
 And I saw their wolf's eyes burn;
I felt like a royal hart at bay,
 And made me ready to turn.
I looked where highest grew the May,
 And deepest arched the fern.

I flew at the first knave's sallow throat;
 One blow, and he was down.
The second rogue fired twice, and missed;
 I sliced the villain's crown,—
Clove through the rest, and flogged brave Kate,
 Fast, fast to Salisbury town!

Pad! pad! they came on the level sward,
 Thud! thud! upon the sand,—
With a gleam of swords and a burning match,
 And a shaking of flag and hand;
But one long bound, and I passed the gate,
 Safe from the canting band.

XIV

Naseby

THIS poem represents the views of a Roundhead soldier who fought in the great civil war between King Charles I of England and the Parliamentary troops under Oliver Cromwell. Naseby is a small village in Northamptonshire, in central England, and one of the most important battles of the war was fought there on June 14, 1645. The Roundheads were led by Cromwell, Lord Fairfax, and General Ireton, and the Cavaliers, or Royal Army, by Prince Rupert. King Charles himself watched the battle from a neighboring hill.

The battle was a defeat for the King's army, and his troops were so badly beaten that the Cavaliers engaged in no more meetings with their foes. Not long afterward Charles became a prisoner of the Parliament, and was tried and beheaded by them in 1649.

The Roundheads were fond of using phrases from the Bible, and the speaker of this poem indulges in many allusions to the Scriptures. His party called themselves the Saints of God, and fought with all the bitter zeal of religious fanatics. He refers most bitterly to the Cavaliers and their leaders, to the " man of blood," King Charles, with his long, curling, perfumed hair, to Lord Astley, who commanded the Royalist infantry, to Sir Marmaduke Langdale, and to Rupert, Prince Palatine of the Rhine. In contrast to these sinful leaders the Roundhead general rode before his troops with the Bible in his hand.

The battle began with the cheers of the two sides. Then Prince Rupert charged, to the sound of clarions and drums, leading, as the Roundhead says, his ruffians from Alsatia, the slums of London, and his lackeys from the King's palace of Whitehall. The Roundheads grasped their pikes and stood manfully, but the charge broke their left wing. Major-General Skippen was wounded, when suddenly Cromwell himself dashed to the rescue of that side of his army. The Roundheads charged behind him, and in their turn broke the Cavalier line. Cromwell pursued; the gallants retreated, trying to save their heads that the Roundheads would like to set up on Temple Bar in London, where the heads of traitors were shown to public view; and King Charles turned and fled.

The speaker calls on his friends to strip lockets and gold from the slain Cavaliers, and then cries shame on the luxury-loving men who were so fond of silks and satins, of music, of theatres, and of cards. He wants to destroy the mitre of the Bishops of the Church of England and the crown of the King, the wickedness of the court and the love of wealth of the Church. Oxford, which sided with Charles, Durham, the seat of a great cathedral, shall be downcast, and both the Roman and the English Church despair.

" Naseby " gives a fine idea of the bigotry and hate

of Cromwell's men for all the pomp and glamour of
King Charles' court and church.

NASEBY

By Thomas Babbington, Lord Macaulay

Oh ! wherefore come ye forth in triumph from the north,
  With your hands, and your feet, and your raiment all red ?
And wherefore doth your rout send forth a joyous shout?
  And whence be the grapes of the wine-press that ye tread ?

Oh ! evil was the root, and bitter was the fruit,
  And crimson was the juice of the vintage that we trod ;
For we trampled on the throng of the haughty and the strong,
  Who sate in the high places and slew the saints of God.

It was about the noon of a glorious day of June,
  That we saw their banners dance and their cuirasses shine,
And the man of blood was there, with his long essenced hair,
  And Astley, and Sir Marmaduke, and Rupert of the Rhine.

Like a servant of the Lord, with his Bible and his sword,
  The general rode along us to form us for the fight ;
When a murmuring sound broke out, and swelled into a shout
  Among the godless horsemen upon the tyrant's right.

And hark ! like the roar of the billows on the shore,
  The cry of battle rises along their charging line :
For God ! for the Cause ! for the Church ! for the laws !
  For Charles, king of England, and Rupert of the Rhine !

The furious German comes, with his clarions and his drums,
 His bravoes of Alsatia and pages of Whitehall;
They are bursting on our flanks! Grasp your pikes! Close
  your ranks!
 For Rupert never comes, but to conquer or to fall.

They are here—they rush on—we are broken—we are gone —
 Our left is borne before them like stubble on the blast.
O Lord, put forth thy might! O Lord, defend the right!
 Stand back to back, in God's name! and fight it to the last!

Stout Skippen hath a wound—the centre hath given ground.
 Hark! Hark! what means the trampling of horsemen on
  our rear?
Whose banner do I see, boys? 'Tis he! thank God! 'tis he,
  boys!
 Bear up another minute! Brave Oliver is here!

Their heads all stooping low, their points all in a row:
 Like a whirlwind on the trees, like a deluge on the dikes,
Our cuirassiers have burst on the ranks of the accurst,
 And at a shock have scattered the forest of his pikes.

Fast, fast, the gallants ride, in some safe nook to hide
 Their coward heads, predestined to rot on Temple Bar;
And he—he turns! he flies! shame on those cruel eyes
 That bore to look on torture, and dare not look on war!

Ho, comrades! scour the plain; and ere ye strip the slain,
 First give another stab to make your search secure;
Then shake from sleeves and pockets their broad-pieces and
  lockets,
 The tokens of the wanton, the plunder of the poor.

Fools ! your doublets shone with gold, and your hearts were
    gay and bold,
  When you kissed your lily hands to your lemans to-day ;
And to-morrow shall the fox from her chambers in the rocks
  Lead forth her tawny cubs to howl above the prey.

Where be your tongues, that late mocked at heaven, and hell,
    and fate ?
  And the fingers that once were so busy with your blades ?
Your perfumed satin clothes, your catches and your oaths ?
  Your stage plays and your sonnets, your diamonds and your
    spades?

Down ! down ! forever down, with the mitre and the crown !
  With the Belial of the court, and the Mammon of the Pope !
There is woe in Oxford halls, there is wail in Durham's stalls ;
  The Jesuit smites his bosom, the bishop rends his cope.

And she of the seven hills shall mourn her children's ills,
  And tremble when she thinks on the edge of England's sword ;
And the kings of earth in fear shall shudder when they hear
  What the hand of God hath wrought for the houses and the
    word !

XV

"Les Gants Glaces"

THE Fronde was the name given to a civil war in France which lasted from 1648 to 1652. The word "fronde" means a "sling" in French, and the war was given that name because it began by the mob of Paris throwing stones at the windows of the houses of the friends of Cardinal Mazarin, who was fighting many of the nobles of France.

Turenne, a great general, led a revolt against Cardinal Mazarin in 1650. Turenne expected to receive aid from the Spaniards in the Netherlands, and a Spanish army was ready to march to join him when the country people of the French province of Champagne took up arms to keep out the foreigners. One of Turenne's allies was holding the town of Rethel, which lay in Ardennes, near the river Vosges. A battle was fought there December 15, 1650, between Turenne's Frondeurs, as his soldiers were called, and the army of Duplessis-Praslin, or, as the name is given in the poem, De Raslin. This poem tells how the attacking army was beaten back from the walls by the Frondeurs, until, goaded with desperation, the weary soldiers taunted the gaily-clad gentlemen of the Household Brigade, who were waiting in reserve, and dared them to advance on the town.

The "Gants Glaces," or "Kid Gloves," as the Brigade was nicknamed, took the challenge, marched forward, and carried the walls, although half their number were swept down in the storm of bullets.

That charge of "Les Gants Glaces" won the day for Cardinal Mazarin and his king, Louis XIV of France.

"LES GANTS GLACES"
Anonymous

Wrapped in smoke stood the towers of Rethel,
  The battle surged fierce by the town;
On terror and struggle and turmoil
  The sweet skies of Champagne looked down.
Far away smiled the beautiful uplands,
  The blue Vosges lay solemn beyond;
Well France knew such discord of color
  In the terrible days of the Fronde.

At the breach in the ramparts of Rethel
  Each stone was bought dearly by blood,
For De Raslin was leading the stormers,
  And Turenne on the battlements stood.
Again and again closed the conflict,
  The madness of strife upon all;
Right well fought the ranks of the marshal,
  Yet twice they fell back from the wall.

Twice, thrice repulsed, baffled, and beaten,
  They glared, where in gallant array,
Brave in gilding and 'broidery and feather,
  The guards in reserve watched the fray.

Go in, ye kid-gloved dandies ! " they shouted
   As sullenly rearward they bore ;
The gaps deep and wide in their columns,
   The lilies all dripping in gore.

Come on, ye kid-gloved dandies ! " and laughing
   At the challenge, the Household Brigade
Dressed ranks, floated standards, blew trumpets,
   And flashed out each glittering blade.
And carelessly as to a banquet,
   And joyously as to a dance,
Where the Frondeurs in triumph were gathered,
   Went the best blood of Scotland and France.

The gay plumes were shorn as in tempest ;
   The gay scarfs stained crimson and black ;
Storm of bullet and broadsword closed o'er them,
   Yet never one proud foot turned back.
Though half of their number lay silent
   On the breach their last effort had won,
King Louis was master of Rethel
   Ere the day and its story was done.

And the fierce taunting cry grew a proverb
   Ere revolt and its horrors were past ;
For men knew, ere o'er France's fair valleys
   Peace waved her banner at last,
That the softest of tones in the boudoir,
   The lightest of steps in the " ronde,"
Was theirs whose keen swords bit the deepest
   In the terrible days of the Fronde.

XVI

How They Brought the Good News from Ghent to Aix

THERE is no actual incident in history such as that described in this poem, but such an adventure might very easily have taken place during one of the wars in the Netherlands. Three riders set out from the city of Ghent, which is in the country now called Belgium, to carry certain news to the town of Aix, in Rhenish Prussia. This news, if it reaches Aix in time, will save that town. The distance to be covered is over a hundred miles.

The three riders, Joris, Dirck, and the one who tells the story, set off from Ghent at full speed, as the moon is setting. The watch opens the city gate, and they gallop out, and race neck and neck mile after mile. Dawn comes as they ride through the towns of Lokeren and Boom and Düffeld. At Mecheln they hear the clock chime. The sun rises at Aerschot. As they near Hasselt Dirck's horse staggers and falls. The other two race on past Looz and Tongres.

As they reach Dalhem Joris cries, "Aix is in sight!" but his roan drops; and the man on Roland is left alone to carry the message. He throws off his coat, and boots, and belt, and urges Roland on. At last they reach Aix, and the noble horse, the hero of the ride, falls as the people crowd about him. The rider, with Roland's head resting between his knees, pours down his steed's throat the last measure of wine left in Aix. The "good news" had arrived in time to save the city.

HOW THEY BROUGHT THE GOOD NEWS FROM GHENT TO AIX

By Robert Browning

I sprang to the stirrup, and Joris and he :
I galloped, Dirck galloped, we galloped all three ;
"Good speed ! " cried the watch as the gate-bolts undrew,
"Speed ! " echoed the wall to us galloping through,
Behind shut the postern, the lights sank to rest,
And into the midnight we galloped abreast.

Not a word to each other ; we kept the great pace —
Neck by neck, stride by stride, never changing our place ;
I turned in my saddle and made its girths tight,
Then shortened each stirrup and set the pique right,
Rebuckled the check-strap, chained slacker the bit,
Nor galloped less steadily Roland a whit.

'Twas a moonset at starting ; but while we drew near
Lokeren, the cocks crew and twilight dawned clear ;
At Boom a great yellow star came out to see ;
At Düffeld 'twas morning as plain as could be ;
And from Mecheln church-steeple we heard the half chime —
So Joris broke silence with " Yet there is time ! "

At Aerschot up leaped of a sudden the sun,
And against him the cattle stood black every one,
To stare through the mist at us galloping past;
And I saw my stout galloper Roland at last,
With resolute shoulders, each butting away
The haze, as some bluff river headland its spray;

And his low head and crest, just one sharp ear bent back
For my voice, and the other pricked out on his track;
And one eye's black intelligence,—ever that glance
O'er its white edge at me, his own master, askance;
And the thick heavy spume-flakes, which aye and anon
His fierce lips shook upward in galloping on.

By Hasselt Dirck groaned; and cried Joris, "Stay spur!
Your Roos galloped bravely, the fault's not in her;
We'll remember at Aix"—for one heard the quick wheeze
Of her chest, saw the stretched neck, and staggering knees,
And sunk tail, and horrible heave of the flank,
As down on her haunches she shuddered and sank.

So we were left galloping, Joris and I,
Past Looz and past Tongres, no cloud in the sky;
The broad sun above laughed a pitiless laugh;
'Neath our feet broke the brittle, bright stubble like chaff;
Till over by Dalhem a dome-spire sprang white,
And "Gallop," gasped Joris, "for Aix is in sight!"

'How they'll greet us!"—and all in a moment his roan
Rolled neck and croup over, lay dead as a stone;
And there was my Roland to bear the whole weight
Of the news which alone could save Aix from her fate,
With his nostrils like pits full of blood to the brim,
And with circles of red for his eye-sockets' rim.

Then I cast loose my buff-coat, each holster let fall,
Shook off both my jack-boots, let go belt and all,
Stood up in the stirrup, leaned, patted his ear,
Called my Roland his pet-name, my horse without peer —
Clapped my hands, laughed and sung, any noise, bad or good,
Till at length into Aix Roland galloped and stood.

And all I remember is friends flocking round,
As I sate with his head 'twixt my knees on the ground ;
And no voice but was praising this Roland of mine,
As I poured down his throat our last measure of wine,
Which (the burgesses voted by common consent)
Was no more than his due who brought good news from Ghent.

XVII

The Bonnets of Bonnie Dundee

SIR WALTER SCOTT loved ballads of the dashing, free-riding, hard-fighting cavaliers, and this is one of the finest that he wrote. The "Bonnets" were the caps of the Scotch horsemen, and Dundee was John Graham of Claverhouse, who was made Viscount of Dundee by James II of England in 1688.

Claverhouse was a leader of wonderful dash and courage, but so cruelly did he treat the Scotch Covenanters against whom he fought that the country people nicknamed him "Bloody Claver'se." When James II was driven from his throne, and William of Orange became King of England Claverhouse planned to raise an army in Scotland and, by defeating the English troops, make James king again. He rode into Edinburgh with his troop of horsemen. The Scottish Parliament, or "Lords of Convention" were assembled there, and he called on them to follow his lead. He bade them open the Westport, or western gate of Edinburgh, and ride forth with him.

But the people of Edinburgh sided with King William, and so the bells were rung backward and the drums sounded to give the alarm. The provost, however, bade the crowd let Claverhouse go, knowing the city would be better off with the wild cavalier safely out of it.

Dundee rode down the turnings of the West Bow, a street where the Scottish Church had met. Every "carline," or old woman, was scolding and shaking her head, but the young girls, the "plants of grace," looked kindly and slyly at him, wishing luck to the dashing soldier.

In the Grass-Market, a famous square of the city, the Whigs, or followers of King William, had gathered, as if half the west of Scotland had come to a hanging. These people had no liking for Claverhouse, but feared his sword. They had pikes and spears and long-handled knives, but they did not dare to attack, and stood close together, leaving the road open to the flaunting troopers.

On a high rock stood Edinburgh Castle, which was held by the Duke of Gordon for King James. Dundee rode to the castle and bade the Duke fire Mons Meg, the great cannon, and the other guns, or "marrows," on the walls. The Duke asked whither he was riding. Dundee answered that he should go wherever the shade of the great Marquis of Montrose, who had fought and died for King Charles II, should lead him. He would go to the country north of the Pentland Hills and the Firth of Forth, and find followers among the wild "Duniewassals", or Scottish chieftains who lived in the Highlands. He would rather live as an outlaw than serve the Whigs' King William, who had usurped King James's throne. So he waved his hand to the castle, and led his men out of the city, riding to the north.

The cause of King James was lost a little later, and

Claverhouse was killed in the battle of Killiecrankie, in 1689.

Sir Walter Scott always preferred the Jacobites to the Whigs, and such a man as Claverhouse, with his " bonnets of Bonnie Dundee," appealed most strongly to his love of romance. The metre of this ballad has the note of galloping horses, flashing swords, and the reckless gaiety of the Cavaliers.

THE BONNETS OF BONNIE DUNDEE
By Sir Walter Scott

To the Lords of Convention 'twas Claverhouse who spoke,
" Ere the king's crown shall fall, there are crowns to be broke ;
So let each cavalier who loves honor and me
Come follow the bonnets of bonnie Dundee ! "

> *Come fill up my cup, come fill up my can ;*
> *Come saddle your horses, and call up your men ;*
> *Come open the Westport and let us gang free,*
> *And it's room for the bonnets of bonnie Dundee !*

Dundee he is mounted, he rides up the street,
The bells are rung backward, the drums they are beat ;
But the provost, douce man, said, " Just e'en let him be,
The gude toun is well quit of that deil of Dundee ! "

As he rode doun the sanctified bends of the Bow,
Ilk carline was flyting and shaking her pow ;
But the young plants of grace they looked cowthie and slee,
Thinking, Luck to thy bonnet, thou bonnie Dundee !

With sour-featured whigs the Grass-Market was thranged,
As if half the west had set tryst to be hanged ;
There was spite in each look, there was fear in each ee,
As they watched for the bonnets of bonnie Dundee.

These cowls of Kilmarnock had spits and had spears,
And lang-hafted gullies to kill cavaliers ;
But they shrunk to close-heads, and the causeway was free
At the toss of the bonnet of bonnie Dundee.

He spurred to the foot of the proud castle rock,
And with the gay Gordon he gallantly spoke :
"Let Mons Meg and her marrows speak twa words or three,
For the love of the bonnet of bonnie Dundee."

The Gordon demands of him which way he goes.
"Where'er shall direct me the shade of Montrose !
Your grace in short space shall hear tidings of me,
Or that low lies the bonnet of bonnie Dundee.

There are hills beyond Pentland and lands beyond Forth ;
If there's lords in the lowlands, there's chiefs in the north ;
There are wild Duniewassals three thousand times three
Will cry ' Hoigh ! ' for the bonnet of bonnie Dundee.

There's brass on the target of barkened bull-hide,
There's steel in the scabbard that dangles beside ;
The brass shall be burnished, the steel shall flash free,
At a toss of the bonnet of bonnie Dundee.

"Away to the hills, to the caves, to the rocks,
Ere I own an usurper I'll couch with the fox :
And tremble, false whigs, in the midst of your glee,
You have not seen the last of my bonnet and me."

He waved his proud hand, and the trumpets were blown,
The kettle-drums clashed, and the horsemen rode on,
Till on Ravelston's cliffs and on Clermiston's lea
Died away the wild war-notes of bonnie Dundee.

> *Come fill up my cup, come fill up my can,*
> *Come saddle the horses, and call up the men;*
> *Come open your doors and let me gae free,*
> *For it's up with the bonnets of bonnie Dundee.*

XVIII

Hervé Riel

THE poet Robert Browning discovered the story of a brave Breton sailor and wrote this poem concerning it. At first it was doubted whether the story was true, but a search of the records of the French navy proved that the facts described actually happened.

The events took place during the war between Louis XIV of France and William III of England in 1692. The French king was fighting the English in order to try to restore James II to his throne. Admiral Tourville, and the French fleet joined battle with the English off Cape La Hogue, and were defeated there May 31, 1692. The French ships were put to flight and headed for the old fortified seaport of St. Malo on the Brittany coast at the mouth of the river Rance.

The great fleet, sailing full in the wind, signaled to St. Malo to give them harbor or the English would take them. The pilots of St. Malo put out in their small boats and reached the fleet, but told the captains it would be impossible to steer such great vessels through the narrow channel and up the shallows of the Rance.

The French captains called a council, and were about to order their ships beached and set on fire rather than surrendered when a simple coasting-pilot, named Hervé Riel, a sailor from the Breton town of La Croisic, who had been pressed into service by Admiral Tourville, stepped out and told them he knew every turn of the channel and could take the fleet through. He asked them to let him steer the biggest ship, the *Formidable*, and he would save them all, or pay the price of failure with his head.

The captains gave the Breton pilot charge, and true to his word he steered the whole fleet up the Rance to safety. The English ships reached the harbor just in time to see the French escape them.

Captains and men cheered Hervé Riel, and Damfreville, in command, told him to name his own reward and, whatever it might be, he should have it. For his great service Hervé Riel simply asked for a day's holiday in order that he might go back to La Croisic to see his wife, whom he called "La Belle Aurore."

To complete his poem Browning says that there is no record of the brave sailor in his native town nor among the heroes of France who are painted in the Louvre at Paris, and offers the tribute of his verse to the daring man who saved the French fleet from the English and for reward asked to see his wife.

Browning wrote this poem at the time when Paris was besieged by the Germans in the winter of 1870–1871. He sent it to the *Cornhill Magazine*, saying they might have it for £100, which he would give to the fund to aid the starving people of Paris. The money was paid him, and given to help the French when the siege had ended.

HERVÉ RIEL
By Robert Browning

I

On the sea and at the Hogue, sixteen hundred ninety-two,
   Did the English fight the French,—woe to France !
And, the thirty-first of May, helter-skelter through the blue,
Like a crowd of frightened porpoises a shoal of sharks pursue,
   Came crowding ship on ship to Saint Malo on the Rance,
With the English fleet in view.

II

'Twas the squadron that escaped, with the victor in full chase ;
   First and foremost of the drove, in his great ship, Damfreville ;
      Close on him fled, great and small,
      Twenty-two good ships in all ;
And they signaled to the place
" Help the winners of a race !
      Get us guidance, give us harbor, take us quick—or, quicker still,
      Here's the English can and will !"

III

Then the pilots of the place put out brisk and leapt on board ;
   " Why, what hope or chance have ships like these to pass ? "
      laughed they :
" Rocks to starboard, rocks to port, all the passage scarred and
      scored,
Shall the *Formidable* here with her twelve and eighty guns
   Think to make the river-mouth by the single narrow way,
Trust to enter where 'tis ticklish for a craft of twenty tons,
      And with flow at full beside ?
      Now, 'tis slackest ebb of tide.
Reach the mooring ?   Rather say,
While rock stands or water runs,
      Not a ship will leave the bay ! "

IV

Then was called a council straight.
Brief and bitter the debate :
" Here's the English at our heels; would you have them take in tow
All that's left us of the fleet, linked together stern and bow,
For a prize to Plymouth Sound ?
Better run the ships aground ! "
     (Ended Damfreville his speech).
" Not a minute more to wait !
     Let the Captains all and each
     Shove ashore, then blow up, burn the vessels on the beach !
France must undergo her fate.

V

" Give the word ! "   But no such word
Was ever spoke or heard ;
     For up stood, for out stepped, for in struck amid all these
—A Captain ?   A Lieutenant ?   A Mate—first, second, third ?
     No such man of mark, and meet
     With his betters to compete !
     But a simple Breton sailor pressed by Tourville for the fleet,
A poor coasting-pilot he, Hervé Riel the Croisickese.

VI

And "What mockery or malice have we here?" cries Hervé Riel :
     "Are you mad, you Malouins ?   Are you cowards, fools, or
          rogues ?
Talk to me of rocks and shoals, me who took the soundings, tell
On my fingers every bank, every shallow, every swell
     'Twixt the offing here and Grève where the river disem-
          bogues ?
Are you bought by English gold ?   Is it love the lying's for ?
     Morn and eve, night and day,
     Have I piloted your bay,
Entered free and anchored fast at the foot of Solidor.

Burn the fleet and ruin France ?   That were worse than fifty
  Hogues !
    Sirs, they know I speak the truth ! Sirs, believe me,
    there's a way !
Only let me lead the line,
  Have the biggest ship to steer,
  Get this *Formidable* clear,
Make the others follow mine,
And I lead them, most and least, by a passage I know well,
  Right to Solidor past Grève,
    And there lay them safe and sound ;
    And if one ship misbehave,
    —Keel so much as grate the ground,
Why, I've nothing but my life,—here's my head ! " cries Hervé
  Riel.

VII

Not a minute more to wait.
" Steer us in, then, small and great !
    Take the helm, lead the line, save the squadron ! " cried its chief.
Captains, give the sailor place !
  He is Admiral, in brief.
Still the north-wind, by God's grace !
See the noble fellow's face
As the big ship, with a bound,
Clears the entry like a hound,
Keeps the passage as its inch of way were the wide sea's profound !
  See, safe through shoal and rock,
  How they follow in a flock,
Not a ship that misbehaves, not a keel that grates the ground,
  Not a spar that comes to grief !
The peril, see, is past,
All are harbored to the last,
And just as Hervé Riel hollas " Anchor ! "—sure as fate,
Up the English come—too late !

VIII

So, the storm subsides to calm :
 They see the green trees wave
 On the heights o'erlooking Grève.
Hearts that bled are stanched with balm.
" Just our rapture to enhance,
 Let the English rake the bay,
Gnash their teeth and glare askance
 As they cannonade away !
'Neath rampired Solidor pleasant riding on the Rance ! "
How hope succeeds despair on each Captain's countenance !
Out burst all with one accord,
  " This is Paradise for Hell !
   Let France, let France's king
   Thank the man that did the thing ! "
What a shout, and all one word,
  " Hervé Riel ! "
As he stepped in front once more,
 Not a symptom of surprise
 In the frank blue Breton eyes,
Just the same man as before.

IX

Then said Damfreville, " My friend,
I must speak out at the end,
 Though I find the speaking hard.
Praise is deeper than the lips :
You have saved the King his ships,
 You must name your own reward.
'Faith our sun was near eclipse !
Demand whate'er you will,
France remains your debtor still.
Ask to heart's content and have ! or my name's not Damfre-
  ville."

X

Then a beam of fun outbroke
On the bearded mouth that spoke,
As the honest heart laughed through
Those frank eyes of Breton blue :
" Since I needs must say my say,
  Since on board the duty's done,
    And from Malo Roads to Croisic Point, what is it but a
        run ? —
Since 'tis ask and have, I may —
  Since the others go ashore —
Come ! A good whole holiday !
  Leave to go and see my wife, whom I call the Belle Aurore ! "
  That he asked and that he got,—nothing more.

XI

Name and deed alike are lost :
Not a pillar nor a post
  In his Croisic keeps alive the feat as it befell ;
Not a head in white and black
On a single fishing-smack,
In memory of the man but for whom had gone to wrack
  All that France saved from the fight whence England bore
      the bell.
Go to Paris : rank on rank
  Search the heroes flung pell-mell
On the Louvre, face and flank !
  You shall look long enough ere you come to Hervé Riel.
So, for better and for worse,
Hervé Riel, accept my verse !
In my verse, Hervé Riel, do thou once more
Save the squadron, honor France, love thy wife the Belle Aurore !

XIX

The Leak in the Dike

A GREAT part of the land of Holland is lower than
the level of the sea about its shores. For this reason
that country and the provinces that adjoin it gained
the name of "The Low Countries," or "The Nether-
lands." In order to keep the sea from flooding their
homes the Hollanders built great walls of earth, called
dikes, and spent large sums of money in repairing
them. The smallest leak was a tremendous danger.
In a very short time it would cause a break in the dike
and let the ocean in to sweep across farms and cities.

Sometimes, when the country was at war with Spain,
or some of the other great powers that tried to conquer
it, the people of Holland would break the dikes them-
selves, and flood their country in order to defeat the
invaders. This was a very costly method of defense,
but several times the brave people had to resort to it.

Alice Cary, an American poet, wrote this poem of
a Dutch boy named Peter. His mother sent him at
sunset one day to carry some cakes to an old man who
lived near the dike. He did the errand, and turned
homeward, stopping to pick some flowers on the way.
As he walked along he heard the angry sea dashing
against the wall that kept it out, and he thought it was

well that the wall was strong and that his father and other men watched it carefully.

Presently he heard a trickling noise. He looked for it, and saw a small stream, not as large as his hand, coming through the dike. He knew what that meant. If it was not stopped the leak would tear down the wall, the sea would sweep in, and destroy hundreds of villages. No one was there to help him, and there was no time to lose. So he pressed his hand to the crack and held it there while he called again and again for aid.

No one came, and Peter had to stay, holding back the sea, while the night passed. His mother wondered what had happened to him, and was up at dawn looking across the fields for him. After a while she saw some neighbors coming toward her, carrying some one. They had found the boy at his post of duty, and they brought him back alive to his mother. By holding the sea outside the dike he had saved his country.

This story has been told many times in prose and poetry. It is one of the legends of Holland that fathers tell their sons when the boys are old enough to understand how the dikes divide the land from the sea.

THE LEAK IN THE DIKE
By Alice Cary

The good dame looked from her cottage
    At the close of the pleasant day,
And cheerily called to her little son
    Outside the door at play:

"Come, Peter, come!   I want you to go,
   While there is light to see,
To the hut of the blind old man who lives
   Across the dike, for me;
And take these cakes I made for him —
   They are hot and smoking yet;
You have time enough to go and come
   Before the sun is set."

Then the good wife turned to her labor,
   Humming a simple song,
And thought of her husband, working hard
   At the sluices all day long;
And set the turf a-blazing,
   And brought the coarse, black bread,
That he might find a fire at night,
   And see the table spread.

And Peter left the brother
   With whom all day he had played,
And the sister who had watched their sports
   In the willow's tender shade;
And told them they'd see him back before
   They saw a star in sight —
Though he wouldn't be afraid to go
   In the very darkest night!
For he was a brave, bright fellow,
   With eye and conscience clear;
He could do whatever a boy might do,
   And he had not learned to fear.
Why, he wouldn't have robbed a bird's nest,
   Nor brought a stork to harm,
Though never a law in Holland
   Had stood to stay his arm!

And now, with his face all glowing,
  And eyes as bright as the day
With the thoughts of his pleasant errand,
  He trudged along the way;
And soon his joyous prattle
  Made glad a lonesome place —
Alas! if only the blind old man
  Could have seen that happy face!
Yet he somehow caught the brightness
  Which his voice and presence lent;
And he felt the sunshine come and go
  As Peter came and went.

And now, as the day was sinking,
  And the winds began to rise,
The mother looked from her door again,
  Shading her anxious eyes,
And saw the shadows deepen,
  And birds to their homes come back,
But never a sign of Peter
  Along the level track.
But she said, "He will come at morning,
  So I need not fret or grieve —
Though it isn't like my boy at all
  To stay without my leave."

But where was the child delaying?
  On the homeward way was he,
And across the dike while the sun was up
  An hour above the sea.
He was stooping now to gather flowers;
  Now listening to the sound,
As the angry waters dashed themselves
  Against their narrow bound.

"Ah ! well for us," said Peter,
    "That the gates are good and strong,
And my father tends them carefully,
    Or they would not hold you long !
You're a wicked sea," said Peter ;
    "I know why you fret and chafe ;
You would like to spoil our lands and homes ;
    But our sluices keep you safe ! "

But hark ! through the noise of waters
    Comes a low, clear, trickling sound ;
And the child's face pales with terror,
    As his blossoms drop to the ground.
He is up the bank in a moment,
    And, stealing through the sand,
He sees a stream not yet so large
    As his slender, childish hand.
'Tis a leak in the dike ! He is but a boy,
    Unused to fearful scenes ;
But, young as he is, he has learned to know
    The dreadful thing that means.
A leak in the dike ! The stoutest heart
    Grows faint that cry to hear,
And the bravest man in all the land
    Turns white with mortal fear.
For he knows the smallest leak may grow
    To a flood in a single night ;
And he knows the strength of the cruel sea
    When loosed in its angry might.

And the boy ! He has seen the danger,
    And, shouting a wild alarm,
He forces back the weight of the sea
    With the strength of his single arm !

He listens for the joyful sound
  Of a footstep passing nigh ;
And lays his ear to the ground, to catch
  The answer to his cry,—
And he hears the rough winds blowing,
  And the waters rise and fall,
But never an answer comes to him
  Save the echo of his call.

He sees no hope, no succor,
  His feeble voice is lost ;
Yet what shall he do but watch and wait,
  Though he perish at his post !
So, faintly calling and crying
  Till the sun is under the sea ;
Crying and moaning till the stars
  Come out for company ;
He thinks of his brother and sister,
  Asleep in their safe warm bed ;
He thinks of dear father and mother ;
  Of himself as dying, and dead ;
And of how, when the night is over,
  They must come and find him at last ;
But he never thinks he can leave the place
  Where duty holds him fast.

The good dame in the cottage
  Is up and astir with the light,
For the thought of her little Peter
  Has been with her all the night.
And now she watches the pathway,
  As yester-eve she had done ;
But what does she see so strange and black
  Against the rising sun ?

Her neighbors are bearing between them
  Something straight to her door ;
Her child is coming home, but not
  As he ever came before !

" He is dead ! " she cries ; " my darling ! "
  And the startled father hears,
And comes and looks the way she looks,
  And fears the thing she fears ;
Till a glad shout from the bearers
  Thrills the stricken man and wife—
" Give thanks, for your son has saved our land,
  And God has saved his life ! "
So, there in the morning sunshine
  They knelt about the boy ;
And every head was bared and bent
  In tearful, reverent joy.

'Tis many a year since then ; but still,
  When the sea roars like a flood,
Their boys are taught what a boy can do
  Who is brave and true and good.
For every man in that country
  Takes his dear son by the hand,
And tells him of little Peter,
  Whose courage saved the land.

They have many a valiant hero,
  Remembered through the years ;
But never one whose name so oft
  Is named with loving tears.
And his deed shall be sung by the cradle,
  And told to the child on the knee,
So long as the dikes of Holland
  Divide the land from the sea !

XX

The Battle of Blenheim

THIS battle was fought near the village of Blenheim, in Bavaria, on the left bank of the river Danube, on August 13, 1704. The French and Bavarians, under Marshals Tallard and Marsin, were defeated by the English and Austrians, under the Duke of Marlborough and Prince Eugene.

The French and Bavarians were taken by surprise in the village, and their armies were badly handled. On the opposite side Marlborough and Prince Eugene showed themselves splendid cavalry leaders and led an attack that proved successful through its very reckless-ness. The French and Bavarians lost 30,000 in killed, wounded, and prisoners, while Marlborough's loss was only 11,000. The battle broke the prestige of the French king, Louis XIV; and when Marlborough re-turned to England his nation built a magnificent man-sion for him and named it Blenheim Palace after this battle.

Southey's poem tells how a little girl found a skull near the battle-field many years afterward, and asked her grandfather how it came there. He told her that a great battle had been fought there, and many of the leaders had won great renown. But he could not tell why it was fought nor what good came of it. He only knew that it was a "great victory." That was the moral of so many of the wars that devastated Europe for centuries. The kings fought for more power and glory; and the peasants fled from burning homes, and the soldiers fell on the fields. The poem gives an idea of the real value to men of such famous victories as that of Blenheim.

THE BATTLE OF BLENHEIM
By Robert Southey

It was a summer evening,
　Old Kaspar's work was done,
And he before his cottage door
　Was sitting in the sun,
And by him sported on the green
His little grandchild Wilhelmine.

She saw her brother Peterkin
　Roll something large and round,
Which he beside the rivulet
　In playing there had found ;
He came to ask what he had found,
That was so large, and smooth, and round.

Old Kaspar took it from the boy,
　Who stood expectant by ;
And then the old man shook his head,
　And with a natural sigh,
" 'Tis some poor fellow's skull," said he,
" Who fell in the great victory.

" I find them in the garden,
　　For there's many here about ;
　And often when I go to plough,
　　The ploughshare turns them out !
　For many thousand men," said he,
" Were slain in that great victory."

" Now tell us what 'twas all about,"
　　Young Peterkin, he cries ;
　And little Wilhelmine looks up
　　With wonder-waiting eyes ;
" Now tell us all about the war,
　And what they fought each other for."

" It was the English," Kaspar cried,
　　" Who put the French to rout ;
　But what they fought each other for
　　I could not well make out ;
　But everybody said," quoth he,
" That 'twas a famous victory.

" My father lived at Blenheim then,
　　Yon little stream hard by ;
　They burnt his dwelling to the ground,
　　And he was forced to fly ;
　So with his wife and child he fled,
　Nor had he where to rest his head.

" With fire and sword the country round
　　Was wasted far and wide,
　And many a childing mother then,
　　And new-born baby died ;
　But things like that, you know, must be
　At every famous victory.

" They say it was a shocking sight
    After the field was won ;
For many thousand bodies here
    Lay rotting in the sun ;
But things like that, you know, must be
After a famous victory.

" Great praise the Duke of Marlbro' won,
    And our good Prince Eugene."
" Why, 'twas a very wicked thing ! "
    Said little Wilhelmine.
" Nay . . . nay . . . my little girl," quoth he,
" It was a famous victory.

" And everybody praised the Duke
    Who this great fight did win."
" But what good came of it at last ? "
    Quoth little Peterkin.
" Why, that I cannot tell," said he,
" But 'twas a famous victory."

XXI

Lochinvar

YOUNG Lochinvar, a gallant of the Border country of Scotland that lies just north of England, rides from his home in the west to seek the maid he loves, the fair Ellen. He goes alone, he pays no heed to bush or stone, he swims the Eske, a river of the Border that flows into Solway Firth, and so comes to Ellen's home, Netherby Castle in England, on the eastern bank of the Eske. But before he could reach the castle the lady Ellen had said she would wed another, a man slow to court her, and backward in war.

The wedding guests were gathered at the castle when Lochinvar entered the hall. The bride's father, hand on sword, demands whether the gallant has come to fight or to dance with the rest. Lochinvar says he comes to dance once with the bride, and drink her one toast. The maid kisses a goblet; he drains it, and throws it away. Then he takes her hand and leads her out into the gay steps of the galliard, while the bridegroom frowns and the guests admire the grace of the two dancers.

They dance to the door. Lochinvar stoops and whispers to the lady. Out at the door they go; he swings her to his charger, vaults up, and away they dash, while after them over the Cannobie meadows ride all of the Netherby clan. But they never caught Lochinvar and his lady.

Sir Walter Scott had matchless skill in writing such ballads as this of the old days in the Border country. He loved every stick and stone of Scotland, and every gallant deed in her history. When he wrote such a poem as this or " The Bonnets of Bonnie Dundee " he struck at once into the dash and glamour of true romance, and the swing of his lines gives the swing of the deeds he describes. His longer poems, " Marmion," " The Lady of the Lake," and "The Lay of the Last Minstrel," give us wonderful pictures of Scotch history, as simple and as glowing as the ballads the troubadours used to sing of famous deeds of chivalry.

" Lochinvar " is a part of the poem of " Marmion."

LOCHINVAR

By Sir Walter Scott

O, young Lochinvar is come out of the west,
Through all the wide border his steed was the best;
And save his good broadsword, he weapon had none,
He rode all unarmed, and he rode all alone.
So faithful in love, and so dauntless in war,
There never was knight like the young Lochinvar.

He staid not for brake, and he stopped not for stone,
He swam the Eske River where ford there was none;
But ere he alighted at Netherby gate,
The bride had consented, the gallant came late:
For a laggard in love, and a dastard in war,
Was to wed the fair Ellen of young Lochinvar.

So boldly he entered the Netherby Hall,
Among bridesmen and kinsmen, and brothers, and all :
Then spake the bride's father, his hand on his sword,
(For the poor craven bridegroom said never a word,)
"O come ye in peace here, or come ye in war,
Or to dance at our bridal, young Lord Lochinvar?"

"I long wooed your daughter, my suit you denied ;
Love swells like the Solway, but ebbs like its tide
And now am I come, with this lost love of mine,
To lead but one measure, drink one cup of wine.
There are maidens in Scotland more lovely by far,
That would gladly be bride to the young Lochinvar."

The bride kissed the goblet : the knight took it up,
He quaffed off the wine, and he threw down the cup.
She looked down to blush, and she looked up to sigh,
With a smile on her lips and a tear in her eye.
He took her soft hand, ere her mother could bar,—
"Now tread we a measure !" said young Lochinvar.

So stately his form, and so lovely her face,
That never a hall such a galliard did grace ;
While her mother did fret, and her father did fume,
And the bridegroom stood dangling his bonnet and plume ;
And the bride-maidens whispered, "'Twere better by far,
To have matched our fair cousin with young Lochinvar."

One touch to her hand, and one word in her ear,
When they reached the hall-door, and the charger stood near ;
So light to the croupe the fair lady he swung,
So light to the saddle before her he sprung.
"She is won ! we are gone over bank, bush and scaur ;
They'll have fleet steeds that follow," quoth young Lochinvar.

There was mounting 'mong Graemes of the Netherby clan;
Forsters, Fenwicks, and Musgraves, they rode and they ran:
There was racing and chasing on Cannobie Lee,
But the lost bride of Netherby ne'er did they see.
So daring in love, and so dauntless in war,
Have ye e'er heard of gallant like young Lochinvar?

XXII

Battle of Fontenoy

FONTENOY is a village of Belgium, and famous as the scene of the battle fought May 11, 1745, between the French under Marshal Saxe and the allied army of English, Dutch, and Austrians, under the Duke of Cumberland. The campaign was part of what is known as the War of the Austrian Succession, which involved almost all the countries of Europe on one side or the other, and which, although it began over a question as to the succession to the throne of Austria, came to have many other objects. At the time of this battle the French were trying to keep the allied army from marching to relieve the siege of the fortress of Tournai.

The French were posted on a hill behind Fontenoy, and at first appeared to have all the advantage. But soon after the battle began the Duke of Cumberland placed himself at the head of his army, and marched a column of fourteen thousand men with fixed bayonets down the ravine between the two forces and up the opposite slope. Legend has it that the advancing English invited the French to fire first, and that the French refused ; but the French were surprised by the brave advance and cheered the enemy. The English then opened a devastating fire, and the first French line broke. The allies charged, and gained the hill. This was the critical moment of the battle. The French king, Louis XV, and the Dauphin, refused to fly, and Marshal Saxe, although ill, mounted his horse and took command of the French cavalry.

The English stood their ground, although the enemy now commenced attacks on three sides. Finally the Irish brigade, allies of the French, charged on the English flank, and after desperate fighting broke the solid English square. The English retreated, but prevented a rout by standing again and again against the terrific onslaughts of the French and Irish. The battle, which at first had appeared likely to be a victory for the allies, ended in a decisive triumph for the French.

The poem is spoken by one of that Irish brigade who had joined the French King Louis and fought England because of the harsh treatment that country had shown Ireland after the battle of the Boyne in 1690.

BATTLE OF FONTENOY
By Bartholomew Dowling

By our camp-fires rose a murmur
　　At the dawning of the day,
And the tread of many footsteps
　　Spoke the advent of the fray ;
And as we took our places,
　　Few and stern were our words,
While some were tightening horse-girths,
　　And some were girding swords.

The Battle of Fontenoy

The trumpet-blast has sounded
    Our footmen to array —
The willing steed has bounded,
    Impatient for the fray —
The green flag is unfolded,
    While rose the cry of joy —
" Heaven speed dear Ireland's banner
    To-day at Fontenoy ! "

We looked upon that banner,
    And the memory arose
Of our homes and perish'd kindred
    Where the Lee or Shannon flows;
We look'd upon that banner,
    And we swore to God on high,
To smite to-day the Saxon's might —
    To conquer or to die.

Loud swells the charging trumpet —
    'Tis a voice from our own land —
God of battles ! God of vengeance !
    Guide to-day the patriot's brand ;
There are stains to wash away,
    There are memories to destroy,
In the best blood of the Briton
    To-day at Fontenoy.

Plunge deep the fiery rowels
    In a thousand reeking flanks —
Down, chivalry of Ireland,
    Down on the British ranks !
Now shall their serried columns
    Beneath our sabres reel —
Through the ranks, then, with the war-horse —
    Through their bosoms with the steel.

With one shout for good King Louis,
 And the fair land of the vine,
Like the wrathful Alpine tempest,
 We swept upon their line —
Then rang along the battle-field
 Triumphant our hurrah,
And we smote them down, still cheering,
 " *Erin, shanthagal go bragh.*"

As prized as is the blessing
 From an aged father's lip —
As welcome as the haven
 To the tempest-driven ship —
As dear as to the lover
 The smile of gentle maid —
Is this day of long-sought vengeance
 To the swords of the Brigade.

See their shatter'd forces flying,
 A broken, routed line —
See, England, what brave laurels
 For your brow to-day we twine.
Oh, thrice bless'd the hour that witness'd
 The Briton turn to flee
From the chivalry of Erin
 And France's "*fleur de lis.*"

As we lay beside our camp-fires,
 When the sun had pass'd away,
And thought upon our brethren
 Who had perished in the fray,
We prayed to God to grant us,
 And then we'd die with joy,
One day upon our own dear land
 Like this of Fontenoy.

XXIII

Bonnie Prince Charlie

"BONNIE PRINCE CHARLIE" was the name affectionately given by certain Scotch and English people to Charles Edward Stuart, son of James Stuart, and grandson of James II, king of England. He was also known as "The Chevalier," or "The Young Pretender," and his father as "The Old Pretender." The Scotch who were still loyal to their old royal house of Stuart claimed that Charles Edward was the rightful king of Great Britain, and wanted to see him take the throne from the House of Hanover.

Prince Charlie landed in Scotland in July, 1745, with only seven friends, and appealed to the chiefs of the Highland clans to give him their aid. "The Old Pretender" had not been a popular leader, but Prince Charlie was young, handsome, and brave, and his love of the Highlands and his dashing manner won the people to his standard. The Highlanders followed him to Edinburgh, where he was proclaimed King James VIII of Scotland. In September, 1745, he won the battle of Preston Pans, and a little later a victory at Falkirk gave him a strong hold on Scotland.

Prince Charlie then marched an army of six thousand men over the border into England, hoping the English would imitate the Scotch. But only a few

English recruits joined him, and the advance of a royal army from the south made him beat a retreat to Scotland. The armies met at the battle of Culloden in Scotland, April 16, 1746, and there the Prince was defeated and forced to fly.

For five months Prince Charlie wandered through the wilds of Scotland, constantly pursued by English soldiers. There was a reward of £30,000 offered for his capture, but the loyal Highlanders sheltered him again and again, and although he was often surrounded by his pursuers he managed to escape them every time. Finally he made his way across to France.

This expedition is known as the rebellion of '45; and it is one of the many romances of Scottish history, due to the dashing gallantry of Prince Charlie and the devotion of the Highlanders. Walter Scott's novel of "Waverly" deals with this story, and many Scotch songs have been sung of "The Young Chevalier."

BONNIE PRINCE CHARLIE
By James Hogg

Cam ye by Athol, lad wi' the philabeg,
  Down by the Tummel, or banks o' the Garry ;
Saw ye our lads, wi' their bonnets and white cockades,
  Leaving their mountains to follow Prince Charlie ?
  Follow thee ! follow thee ! wha wadna follow thee ?
    Lang hast thou loved and trusted us fairly :
Charlie, Charlie, wha wadna follow thee,
    King o' the Highland hearts, bonnie Prince Charlie ?

I hae but ae son, my gallant young Donald ;
   But if I had ten, they should follow Glengary.
Health to M'Donnel, and gallant Clan-Ronald,
    For these are the men that will die for their Charlie!
    Follow thee ! follow thee ! wha wadna follow thee?
      Lang hast thou loved and trusted us fairly:
    Charlie, Charlie, wha wadna follow thee,
      King o' the Highland hearts, bonnie Prince Charlie ?

I'll to Lochiel and Appin, and kneel to them,
   Down by Lord Murray, and Roy of Kildarlie ;
Brave M'Intosh he shall fly to the field with them ;
    These are the lads I can trust wi' my Charlie !
    Follow thee ! follow thee ! wha wadna follow thee?
      Lang hast thou loved and trusted us fairly:
    Charlie, Charlie, wha wadna follow thee,
      King o' the Highland hearts, bonnie Prince Charlie ?

Down through the Lowlands, down wi' the Whigamore !
   Loyal true Highlanders, down wi' them rarely !
Ronald and Donald, drive on wi' the broad claymore,
    Over the necks of the foes of Prince Charlie !
    Follow thee ! follow thee ! wha wadna follow thee?
      Lang hast thou loved and trusted us fairly:
    Charlie, Charlie, wha wadna follow thee,
      King o' the Highland hearts, bonnie Prince Charlie ?

XXIV

Boston

RALPH WALDO EMERSON had planned to write a poem about his native city of Boston for many years, and some of the lines in the finished poem were thought out long before he composed the verses as they stand. Emerson read the poem on December 16, 1873, in Faneuil Hall, on the One Hundredth Anniversary of the destruction of the tea in Boston Harbor. The Latin words that he placed at the beginning, and which are the motto of Boston, he translated " God with the Fathers, So with Us."

Boston, settled by good Puritan stock, was one of the first cities in the thirteen colonies to resist the unfair rule of England. Patriots in most of the other cities had let it be known that they would unite in the common cause, but the men of Boston had to begin the contest. They claimed that England was taxing the colonies without allowing them any chance to be heard in parliament, and they especially complained of the tax on all tea that was brought into the port. But the more the colonists objected the more the King of England insisted on proving his rights to them. Therefore he sent several ships loaded with tea to America in the autumn of 1773. The first ship reached Boston Harbor Sunday, November 28th, and a few days later two others arrived. The citizens were furious at this attempt to make them pay the tax on tea, and held town-meetings, and voted to do without tea.

The people became more and more indignant, and finally ordered the captains of the vessels laden with tea to leave the port. The captains agreed, but failed to sail. Finally the men of Boston planned to settle the difficulty for themselves. On the evening of December 16, 1773, a band of forty or fifty men, clad in blankets like Indians, with hatchets in their hands, met at a church. From there they marched to Griffin's Wharf, recruits joining them on the way, until they numbered nearly two hundred. They posted guards on the wharf, and then boarded the three tea-ships. In three hours the band had broken open the three hundred and forty chests of tea that were on board, and emptied them into the harbor. Nothing else on the ships was touched, and as soon as the work was done the men went quietly to their homes. But that very night men of the near-by villages received word of the "Boston Tea-Party," and the next morning couriers were sent to the other colonies to give an account of the stand Boston had taken.

News of the Tea-Party caused great indignation in England, and the King ordered that no ships should be allowed to enter the port of Boston until that town should have paid the East India Company for the lost tea. The charter of Massachusetts was annulled, and General Gage was sent over from England with four regiments to take possession of the rebellious city and keep it in order.

But the spirit of Boston was the spirit of independence, and the men who had thrown the tea overboard were soon afterwards to withstand the British fire at Lexington and Concord.

BOSTON

By Ralph Waldo Emerson
(*Sicut Patribus, sit Deus Nobis*)

The rocky nook with hilltops three
　　Looked eastward from the farms,
And twice each day the flowing sea
　　　Took Boston in its arms;
　　　　The men of yore were stout and poor,
　　　　And sailed for bread to every shore.

And where they went on trade intent
　　They did what freeman can,
Their dauntless ways did all men praise,
　　　The merchant was a man.
　　　　The world was made for honest trade,—
　　　　To plant and eat be none afraid.

The waves that rocked them on the deep
　　To them their secret told;
Said the winds that sung the lads to sleep,
　　　" Like us be free and bold!"
　　　　The honest waves refuse to slaves
　　　　The empire of the ocean caves.

Old Europe groans with palaces,
　　Has lords enough and more;—
We plant and build by foaming seas
　　　A city of the poor;—
　　　　For day by day could Boston Bay
　　　　Their honest labor overpay.

We grant no dukedoms to the few,
　　We hold like rights and shall ;—
Equal on Sunday in the pew,
　　On Monday in the mall.
　　　　For what avail the plough or sail,
　　　　Or land or life, if freedom fail ?

The noble craftsmen we promote,
　　Disown the knave and fool ;
Each honest man shall have his vote,
　　Each child shall have his school.
　　　　A union then of honest men,
　　　　Or union nevermore again.

The wild rose and the barberry thorn
　　Hung out their summer pride
Where now on heated pavements worn
　　The feet of millions stride.

Fair rose the planted hills behind
　　The good town on the bay,
And where the western hills declined
　　The prairie stretched away.

What care though rival cities soar
　　Along the stormy coast :
Penn's town, New York, and Baltimore,
　　If Boston knew the most !

They laughed to know the world so wide ;
　　The mountains said : "Good-day !
We greet you well, you Saxon men,
　　Up with your towns and stay ! "
　　　　The world was made for honest trade,—
　　　　To plant and eat be none afraid.

" For you," they said, "no barriers be,
  For you no sluggard rest;
Each street leads downward to the sea,
  Or landward to the West."

O happy town beside the sea,
  Whose roads lead everywhere to all;
Than thine no deeper moat can be,
  No stouter fence, no steeper wall!

Bad news from George on the English throne:
  "You are thriving well," said he;
" Now by these presents be it known,
  You shall pay us a tax on tea;
    'Tis very small,—no load at all,—
    Honor enough that we send the call."

" Not so," said Boston, "good my lord,
  We pay your governors here
Abundant for their bed and board,
  Six thousand pounds a year.
(Your highness knows our homely word,)
    Millions for self-government,
    But for tribute never a cent."

The cargo came! and who could blame
  If *Indians* seized the tea,
And, chest by chest, let down the same
  Into the laughing sea?
    For what avail the plough or sail
    Or land or life, if freedom fail?

The townsmen braved the English king,
  Found friendship in the French,
And Honor joined the patriot ring
  Low on their wooden bench.

O bounteous seas that never fail !
  O day remembered yet !
O happy port that spied the sail
  Which wafted Lafayette !
    Pole-star of light in Europe's night,
    That never faltered from the right.

Kings shook with fear, old empires crave
  The secret force to find
Which fired the little State to save
  The rights of all mankind.

But right is might through all the world ;
  Province to province faithful clung,
Through good and ill the war-bolt hurled,
  Till Freedom cheered and the joy-bells rung.

The sea returning day by day
  Restores the world-wide mart ;
So let each dweller on the Bay
  Fold Boston in his heart,
    Till these echoes be choked with snows,
    Or over the town blue ocean flows.

XXV

Paul Revere's Ride

ALL during the winter of 1774–75 an armed truce
had existed between the British officials and army in
the colony of Massachusetts and the people. No citi-
zen could be found who would serve as councillor,
judge, sheriff, or juryman under the King's commis-
sion, and the official business of the colony was at a
standstill. Every evening the men of each village
drilled on the green, and arms and ammunition were
collected secretly and stored in town-halls ready for
instant use in the conflict which every one expected.
The colonials intended that England should be forced
to fire the opening shot, so that they would be in the
position of defending their homes rather than of at-
tacking the King's government. Gradually a large
supply of powder and ball was stored at Concord,
about eighteen miles away from Boston, and word of
this at length came to General Gage, who commanded
the British troops in the latter city.

At about the same time General Gage received
orders to arrest two men who had shown themselves
leaders among the colonials, Samuel Adams and John
Hancock. They were to be sent to England to stand
trial for treason. He learned that the two men would
be in Lexington at a friend's house during the middle of

April, and gave commands that a detachment of eight hundred troops should march from Boston to Lexington, take Adams and Hancock prisoners, and then march on to Concord, which lay beyond Lexington, and seize the stores of powder and shot there.

The British soldiers started on their march on the night of April 18, 1775, keeping their plans as secret as possible, and crossing from Boston to Cambridge, on their way to Concord. In spite of their care, however, word of the plans had leaked out, and the colonial leaders in Boston selected Paul Revere and William Dawes to ride with the news.

It had been arranged that Paul Revere should wait in Charlestown, opposite Boston, until he should see a lantern shining in the tower of the old North Church. When he caught the signal he mounted a swift horse and galloped out of Charlestown on the road to Lexington. As he rode he waked the country people, and they knew that the British troops were on the march. He reached Lexington in time to give the warning to Adams and Hancock, so that they escaped. William Dawes, who had ridden with the same news by way of Roxbury, and Dr. Samuel Prescott, rode on with Paul Revere. They met some British soldiers at Lincoln, but Prescott leaped his horse over a roadside wall and escaped, to take the alarm to Concord. Revere and Dawes were made prisoners, but were soon released.

The British soldiers reached Concord and destroyed a large part of the supplies there, but by the time they began their return to Boston the minutemen were roused. The indignant farmers fired, to the amaze-

ment of the red-coated soldiers, and soon the British
march became a retreat, and almost a rout.   Reinforce-
ments were sent to their aid before they reached Boston,
and but for that very few would have escaped their
pursuers.   As it was, this first fight of the War for
American Independence was a victory for the colonials.

This poem is the "Landlord's Tale," the first of the
"Tales of a Wayside Inn."

PAUL REVERE'S RIDE

By Henry Wadsworth Longfellow

Listen, my children, and you shall hear
Of the midnight ride of Paul Revere,
On the eighteenth of April, in Seventy-Five:
Hardly a man is now alive
Who remembers that famous day and year.

He said to his friend, "If the British march
By land or sea from the town to-night,
Hang a lantern aloft in the belfry arch
Of the North Church tower as a signal light,
One, if by land, and two, if by sea;
And I on the opposite shore will be,
Ready to ride and spread the alarm
Through every Middlesex village and farm,
For the country folk to be up and to arm."

Then he said, Good-night! and with muffled oar
Silently rowed to the Charlestown shore,
Just as the moon rose over the bay,
Where swinging wide at her moorings lay

The *Somerset*, British man-of-war ;
A phantom ship, with each mast and spar
Across the moon like a prison-bar,
And a huge black hulk, that was magnified
By its own reflection in the tide.

Meanwhile, his friend, through alley and street,
Wanders and watches, with eager ears,
Till in the silence around him he hears
The muster of men at the barrack door,
The sound of arms, and the tramp of feet,
And the measured tread of the grenadiers,
Marching down to their boats on the shore.

Then he climb'd to the tower of the old North
     Church,
By the wooden stairs, with stealthy tread,
To the belfry-chamber overhead,
And startled the pigeons from their perch
On the sombre rafters, that round him made
Masses and moving shapes of shade ;
By the trembling ladder, steep and tall,
To the highest window in the wall,
Where he paused to listen and look down
A moment on the roofs of the town,
And the moonlight flowing over all.

Beneath, in the churchyard, lay the dead
In their night-encampment on the hill,
Wrapp'd in silence so deep and still,
That he could hear, like a sentinel's tread,
The watchful night-wind, as it went
Creeping along from tent to tent,
And seeming to whisper, " All is well ! "
A moment only he feels the spell

Of the place and the hour, and the secret dread
Of the lonely belfry and the dead ;
For suddenly all his thoughts are bent
On a shadowy something far away,
Where the river widens to meet the bay,—
A line of black, that bends and floats
On the rising tide, like a bridge of boats.

Meanwhile, impatient to mount and ride,
Booted and spurr'd, with a heavy stride,
On the opposite shore walk'd Paul Revere.
Now he patted his horse's side,
Now gazed at the landscape far and near,
Then, impetuous, stamp'd the earth,
And turn'd and tighten'd his saddle-girth ;
But mostly he watch'd with eager search
The belfry-tower of the old North Church,
As it rose above the graves on the hill,
Lonely, and spectral, and sombre and still.
And lo ! as he looks, on the belfry's height
A glimmer, and then a gleam of light !
He springs to the saddle, the bridle he turns,
But lingers and gazes, till full on his sight
A second lamp in the belfry burns !

A hurry of hoofs in a village street,
A shape in the moonlight, a bulk in the dark,
And beneath, from the pebbles, in passing, a spark
Struck out by a steed flying fearless and fleet :
That was all !   And yet, through the gloom and the
    light,
The fate of a nation was riding that night ;
And the spark struck out by that steed, in his flight,
Kindled the land into flame with its heat.

He has left the village and mounted the steep,
And beneath him, tranquil and broad and deep,
Is the Mystic, meeting the ocean tides;
And under the alders that skirt its edge,
Now soft on the sand, now loud on the ledge,
Is heard the tramp of his steed as he rides.

It was twelve by the village clock,
When he crossed the bridge into Medford town.
He heard the crowing of the cock,
And the barking of the farmer's dog,
And felt the damp of the river fog,
That rises after the sun goes down.

It was one by the village clock,
When he galloped into Lexington.
He saw the gilded weathercock
Swim in the moonlight as he passed,
And the meeting-house windows, blank and bare,
Gaze at him with a spectral glare,
As if they already stood aghast
At the bloody work they would look upon.

It was two by the village clock,
When he came to the bridge in Concord town.
He heard the bleating of the flock,
And the twitter of birds among the trees,
And felt the breath of the morning breeze
Blowing over the meadows brown.
And one was safe and asleep in his bed
Who at the bridge would be first to fall,
Who that day would be lying dead,
Pierced by a British musket-ball.

You know the rest.   In the books you have read
How the British regulars fired and fled ;
How the farmers gave them ball for ball,
From behind each fence and farmyard-wall,
Chasing the redcoats down the lane,
Then crossing the fields to emerge again
Under the trees at the turn of the road,
And only pausing to fire and load.

So through the night rode Paul Revere ;
And so through the night went his cry of alarm
To every Middlesex village and farm,—
A cry of defiance, and not of fear,—
A voice in the darkness, a knock at the door,
And a word that shall echo forevermore !
For, borne on the night-wind of the Past,
Through all our history, to the last,
In the hour of darkness, and peril, and need,
The people will waken and listen to hear
The hurrying hoof-beat of that steed,
And the midnight message of Paul Revere.

XXVI

The Battle of Lexington

PAUL REVERE had wakened the little town of Lexington at midnight of April 18, 1775, with word that General Gage and the British regulars were on the march to seize the stores at Concord. William Dawes had brought the same message, riding through Roxbury. Then Dawes and Revere and Samuel Prescott rode on until they reached Lincoln, where the first two were captured by the British, but Prescott escaped to Concord.

In 1775 there may have been some seven hundred people in Lexington. By two in the morning of April 19th, Lexington Common was filled with minutemen. The roll was called, and one hundred and thirty answered to their names. Then the captain, John Parker, ordered every man to load his musket with powder and ball, but not to be the first to fire. Messengers, who had been sent out to look for the British troops, reported they were not in sight, so the company was dismissed with orders to come together instantly at the sound of a drum.

Dawn was just breaking when the first British soldiers were seen advancing along the road. The drums called the minutemen together, and the raw soldiers were drawn up in two ranks, near the north side of the meeting-house.

The British, hearing the drums and signal-guns, halted and loaded their muskets. Then the advance guard, led by Major Pitcairn, and followed by the grenadiers, went forward at the double-quick. When Pitcairn was near the minutemen he cried out: " Disperse, ye villains ! ye rebels, disperse ! lay down your arms ! why don't you lay down your arms and disperse ? "

Although the minutemen were far fewer than the British soldiers they stood their ground. Pitcairn fired his pistol, and called to his men, " Fire ! " A few guns answered, and then followed a deadly discharge of muskets at short range.

Captain Parker, seeing that his men were too few to withstand so many, ordered them to retreat. Then a few of them, of their own accord, fired at the regulars, but did them no harm. Seven men of Lexington, however, were killed by the British fire, and nine wounded. Jonas Parker had sworn never to run from British troops; he stood his ground and was stabbed by a bayonet as he reloaded his gun. Robert Munroe, a veteran of earlier wars, was killed. Samuel Hadley and John Brown were followed and shot down after they had left the common, and Asahel Porter, who had been captured and was trying to escape, was also shot. Caleb Harrington, who had gone to the meeting-house for powder, was killed by a bullet as he came out, and Jonathan Harrington, Jr., was struck in front of his own house on the common. His wife was at the window. He fell, then got to his knees, and crawled to his doorstep. There he died as his wife reached him.

The Battle of Lexington

Daylight found Lexington Common stained with blood, and seven of the town's brave sons dead. Yet Samuel Adams, looking into the future, could exclaim, "Oh, what a glorious morning is this!" for he knew that the heroic stand of that little company was the first step towards the winning of their country's independence.

This poem by Sidney Lanier is a part of a longer poem called "Psalm of the West."

THE BATTLE OF LEXINGTON
By Sidney Lanier
(From the "Psalm of the West.")

Now haste thee while the way is clear,
    Paul Revere!
Haste, Dawes! but haste thou not, O Sun!
    To Lexington.

Then Devens looked and saw the light:
He got him forth into the night,
And watched alone on the river-shore,
And marked the British ferrying o'er.

John Parker! rub thine eyes and yawn:
But one o'clock and yet 'tis Dawn!
Quick, rub thine eyes and draw thy hose:
The Morning comes ere darkness goes,
Have forth and call the yeomen out,
For somewhere, somewhere close about
Full soon a Thing must come to be
Thine honest eyes shall stare to see
Full soon before thy patriot eyes
Freedom from out of a Wound shall rise.

Then haste ye, Prescott and Revere !
Bring all the men of Lincoln here ;
Let Chelmsford, Littleton, Carlisle,
Let Acton, Bedford, hither file —
Oh hither file, and plainly see
Out of a wound leap Liberty.

Say, Woodman April ! all in green,
Say, Robin April ! hast thou seen
In all thy travel round the earth
Ever a morn of calmer birth ?
But Morning's eye alone serene
Can gaze across yon village-green
To where the trooping British run
　　　　Through Lexington.

Good men in fustian, stand ye still ;
The men in red come o'er the hill.
Lay down your arms, damned Rebels ! cry
The men in red full haughtily.
But never a grounding gun is heard ;
The men in fustian stand unstirred ;
Dead calm, save maybe a wise bluebird
Puts in his little heavenly word.

O men in red ! if ye but knew
The half as much as bluebirds do,
Now in this little tender calm
Each hand would out, and every palm
With patriot palm strike brotherhood's stroke
Or ere these lines of battle broke.

O men in red ! if ye but knew
The least of the all that bluebirds do,
Now in this little godly calm
Yon voice might sing the Future's Psalm —

The Psalm of Love with the brotherly eyes
Who pardons and is very wise —
Yon voice that shouts, high-hoarse with ire,
      Fire !

The redcoats fire, the homespuns fall:
The homespuns' anxious voices call,
Brother, art hurt ? and *Where hit, John ?*
And, *Wipe this blood,* and *Men, come on,*
And *Neighbor, do but lift my head,*
And *Who is wounded ? Who is dead ?*
Seven are killed. My God ! my God !
Seven lie dead on the village sod.
Two Harringtons, Parker, Hadley, Brown,
Munroe and Porter,—these are down.
Nay, look ! stout Harrington not yet dead !
He crooks his elbow, lifts his head.
He lies at the step of his own house-door ;
He crawls and makes a path of gore.
The wife from the window hath seen, and rushed ;
He hath reached the step, but the blood hath gushed ;
He hath crawled to the step of his own house-door,
But his head hath dropped : he will crawl no more.
Clasp, Wife, and kiss, and lift the head :
Harrington lies at his door-step dead.

But, O ye Six that round him lay
And bloodied up that April day !
As Harrington fell, ye likewise fell —
At the door of the House wherein ye dwell ;
As Harrington came, ye likewise came
And died at the door of your House of Fame.

XXVII

Concord Hymn

THIS poem was written to be sung as a hymn at the completion of the monument erected on the bank of the Concord River in Massachusetts April 19, 1836. It was there that the colonial minutemen withstood the British regulars on April 19, 1775, and, as Emerson says, "fired the shot heard round the world," beginning the War of American Independence.

Emerson's grandfather, William Emerson, was a minister at Concord in 1775, and had strongly urged resistance to the British in his sermons. He himself stood with the farmers by the bridge, saying to the minutemen, "Let us stand our ground. If we die, let us die here."

The battle took place near the minister's own house, which was afterwards the home of his grandson, Ralph Waldo Emerson, and of Nathaniel Hawthorne. Hawthorne gave it fame as "The Old Manse" of his writings.

CONCORD HYMN
By Ralph Waldo Emerson

By the rude bridge that arched the flood,
    Their flag to April's breeze unfurled,
Here once the embattled farmers stood,
    And fired the shot heard round the world.

The foe long since in silence slept;
  Alike the conqueror silent sleeps;
And Time the ruined bridge has swept
  Down the dark stream which seaward creeps.

On this green bank, by this soft stream,
  We set to-day a votive stone;
That memory may their deed redeem,
  When, like our sires, our sons are gone.

Spirit, that made those heroes dare
  To die, and leave their children free,
Bid Time and Nature gently spare
  The shaft we raise to them and thee.

XXVIII

The Green Mountain Boys

SOON after the first armed encounters between the British troops stationed in Boston under General Gage and the minutemen of Lexington and Concord and other villages, a large army of recruits collected outside Boston. There were nearly twenty thousand of these men who had hurriedly left homes and farms and hastened to besiege General Gage and his regulars. The leaders, however, did not consider the time ripe to attack such a strong British force. The recruits were eager and warlike, and it was soon seen that their martial spirit must be given some outlet. It was then that Benedict Arnold, captain of a volunteer company from Connecticut, suggested that a march be made against the British fortresses at Ticonderoga and Crown Point, on Lake Champlain. These were of great strategic value, as they commanded the approach to the Hudson River on the north.

This idea met with a quick response. Arnold was made a colonel, and started to raise a regiment among the colonists in the Berkshire Hills. Meantime, however, a number of other men were raising recruits in the country which was known as the New Hampshire Grants, now the state of Vermont. Ethan Allen was one of the leaders here, and while some of the captains were on the march from Boston, he sent an alarm from the town of Bennington through the hills and valleys of the Green Mountain country. The settlers came hurriedly at his call, and on May 7, 1775, one hundred Green Mountain Boys, as these patriots were called, and about fifty men from Massachusetts, met at Castleton. Benedict Arnold joined them, but, although he already had a military commission from the Massachusetts committee of safety, the recruits disregarded his claim, and unanimously elected Ethan Allen their commander.

The fortress of Ticonderoga was strongly guarded with cannon, and the Green Mountain Boys knew that if they were to capture it they would have to take the British garrison by surprise. As secretly as they could, therefore, they set out from Castleton, heading for Lake Champlain. On May ninth they camped at Orwell, and planned to make their attack on the next day.

THE GREEN MOUNTAIN BOYS
By William Cullen Bryant

Here halt we our march, and pitch our tent
  On the rugged forest-ground,
And light our fire with the branches rent
  By winds from the beeches round.
Wild storms have torn this ancient wood,
  But a wilder is at hand,
With hail of iron and rain of blood,
  To sweep and waste the land.

How the dark wood rings with our voices shrill,
    That startle the sleeping bird !
To-morrow eve must the voice be still,
    And the step must fall unheard.
The Briton lies by the blue Champlain,
    In Ticonderoga's towers,
And ere the sun rise twice again,
    Must they and the lake be ours.

Fill up the bowl from the brook that glides
    Where the fireflies light the brake ;
A ruddier juice the Briton hides
    In his fortress by the lake.
Build high the fire, till the panther leap
    From his lofty perch in flight,
And we'll strengthen our weary arms with sleep
    For the deeds of to-morrow night.

XXIX

Ticonderoga

THE Green Mountain Boys, led by Ethan Allen, and accompanied by Benedict Arnold as a volunteer, managed to collect a few boats at Orwell, and eighty-three of the men crossed Lake Champlain early in the morning of May 10, 1775, and landed at Ticonderoga. The boats were sent back for the rest of the expedition, but the commander realized that if he was to take the enemy by surprise he could not wait until the others arrived. Dawn was just breaking over the mountains as Ethan Allen drew up his little band in ranks. According to history he said to them, " Friends and fellow-soldiers, we must this morning quit our pretentions to valor, or possess ourselves of this fortress ; and, inasmuch as it is a desperate attempt, I do not urge it on, contrary to will. You that will undertake voluntarily, poise your firelock."

Every man raised his firelock. " Face to the right ! " cried Allen. He took his place at the head of the centre file, and with Arnold beside him, led the march to the gate of the fortress. The gate was shut, but the wicket in it was open. A sentry fired through it, and then the Americans broke down the gate and dashed upon the few guards and captured them. The attackers raised the old Indian war-whoops of the days of Montcalm, and quickly formed a hollow square on the parade ground, one side facing each of the barracks. One of the sentries showed Allen the door of the British commander's room. " Come out instantly, or I will sacrifice the whole garrison ! " cried Ethan Allen. Delaplace, the British commander, jumped out of bed and gazed in amazement at the American. " Deliver to me the fort instantly," said the American. " By what authority ? " asked the British officer. " In the name of the great Jehovah, and the Continental Congress ! " answered Ethan Allen.

Delaplace started to speak, but Allen threatened him with his drawn sword, and called for his surrender. Then the commander capitulated, and ordered the garrison to give up their arms. By this sudden attack a few almost undisciplined volunteer soldiers won in about ten minutes a fortress that had caused the British troops many campaigns against the French and Indians. The Green Mountain Boys took a large number of prisoners at Ticonderoga, more than one hundred pieces of cannon, and stores of powder and arms. They sent a band of their men to the other fortress of Crown Point, and took that as easily as they had captured the larger and more important one.

Coming as it did, at the very beginning of the War of Revolution, the success of the Green Mountain Boys gave the greatest cheer to the colonists from Massachusetts to Georgia.

The Capture of Fort Ticonderoga

TICONDEROGA
By V. B. Wilson

The cold, gray light of the dawning
   On old Carillon falls,
And dim in the mist of the morning
   Stand the grim old fortress walls.
No sound disturbs the stillness
   Save the cataract's mellow roar,
Silent as death is the fortress,
   Silent the misty shore.

But up from the wakening waters
   Comes the cool, fresh morning breeze,
Lifting the banner of Britain,
   And whispering to the trees
Of the swift gliding boats on the waters
   That are nearing the fog-shrouded land,
With the old Green Mountain Lion,
   And his daring patriot band.

But the sentinel at the postern
   Heard not the whisper low ;
He is dreaming of the banks of Shannon
   As he walks on his beat to and fro,
Of the starry eyes in Green Erin
   That were dim when he marched away,
And a tear down his bronzed cheek courses,
   'Tis the first for many a day.

A sound breaks the misty stillness,
   And quickly he glances around ;
Through the mist, forms like towering giants
   Seem rising out of the ground ;

A challenge, the firelock flashes,
  A sword cleaves the quivering air,
And the sentry lies dead by the postern,
  Blood staining his bright yellow hair.

Then, with a shout that awakens
  All the echoes of hillside and glen,
Through the low, frowning gate of the fortress,
  Sword in hand, rush the Green Mountain men.
The scarce wakened troops of the garrison
  Yield up their trust pale with fear;
And down comes the bright British banner,
  And out rings a Green Mountain cheer.

Flushed with pride, the whole eastern heavens
  With crimson and gold are ablaze ;
And up springs the sun in his splendor
  And flings down his arrowy rays,
Bathing in sunlight the fortress,
  Turning to gold the grim walls,
While louder and clearer and higher
  Rings the song of the waterfalls.

Since the taking of Ticonderoga
  A century has rolled away ;
But with pride the nation remembers
  That glorious morning in May.
And the cataract's silvery music
  Forever the story tells,
Of the capture of old Carillon,
  The chime of the silver bells.

XXX

The Little Black-Eyed Rebel

THE British troops under General Howe made Philadelphia their headquarters during the winter of 1777–1778. They entered that city, which was the largest and most important in the thirteen states, on September 26, 1777, having defeated Washington's army in a series of small engagements. The American commander-in-chief withdrew to a safe distance from the city, and prepared to rest and recruit his forces before meeting Howe again.

In the meantime the British General Burgoyne had surrendered at Saratoga, and many troops that had been engaged in fighting him joined Washington's command. By November, 1777, there was a general clamor for Washington to capture Philadelphia. But that city was protected by the Schuylkill and Delaware Rivers and could only be approached from the north, and on that side the British had built a chain of fourteen redoubts. Washington realized that his army would have little chance of taking the city from the large British force there, and selected the woods of Whitemarsh for a temporary encampment.

General Howe in Philadelphia heard that the Americans were ill prepared for an attack, and so, on December fourth, he marched fourteen thousand men against them. Washington, with only some seven thousand really effective soldiers, prepared to meet him, but after much manœuvering and several slight skirmishes Howe decided that the Americans were too well protected by the broken country and their entrenchments, and retired into the city again. The rest of the winter Howe spent in Philadelphia, and Washington put his army into winter quarters at Valley Forge, on the Schuylkill River, twenty-one miles outside of Philadelphia. Thus the two armies rested, and waited for spring to renew hostilities. When spring came, to the surprise of the Tories, the British marched out of the city on June 18, 1778, and allowed the Americans to enter unmolested.

The British spent the winter in Philadelphia in entertainments of every fashion; the Americans at Valley Forge had difficulty in getting sufficient food and clothing. With the army so near it was natural that many of the soldiers should try to send messages to their families in the city, and receive word from them. Many plans were tried to dodge the British sentries, and letters were often hidden in the farm-wagons that drove into town with provisions for citizens and soldiers.

One of those who was most active in sending messages was a Philadelphia girl named Mary Redmond. She was known as " The Little Black-eyed Rebel," and Will Carleton's poem tells the true story of one of her successful attempts to smuggle notes from the soldiers at Valley Forge to their wives and children in Philadelphia.

THE LITTLE BLACK-EYED REBEL
By Will Carleton
[From *Poems For Young Americans*, by Will Carleton]

A boy drove into the city, his wagon loaded down
With food to feed the people of the British-governed town ;
And the little black-eyed rebel, so innocent and sly,
Was watching for his coming from the corner of her eye.

His face looked broad and honest, his hands were brown and tough,
The clothes he wore upon him were homespun, coarse, and rough ;
But one there was who watched him, who long time lingered nigh,
And cast at him sweet glances from the corner of her eye.

He drove up to the market, he waited in the line ;
His apples and potatoes were fresh and fair and fine ;
But long and long he waited, and no one came to buy,
Save the black-eyed rebel, watching from the corner of her eye.

"Now who will buy my apples?" he shouted, long and loud ;
And "Who wants my potatoes?" he repeated to the crowd ;
But from all the people round him came no word of a reply,
Save the black-eyed rebel, answering from the corner of her eye.

For she knew that 'neath the lining of the coat he wore that day,
Were long letters from the husbands and the fathers far away,
Who were fighting for the freedom that they meant to gain or die ;
And a tear like silver glistened in the corner of her eye.

But the treasures—how to get them ? crept the question through
    her mind,
Since keen enemies were watching for what prizes they might find :
And she paused a while and pondered, with a pretty little sigh ;
Then resolve crept through her features, and a shrewdness fired
    her eye.

So she resolutely walked up to the wagon old and red ;
" May I have a dozen apples for a kiss ? " she sweetly said :
And the brown face flushed to scarlet ; for the boy was somewhat
    shy,
And he saw her laughing at him from the corner of her eye.

" You may have them all for nothing, and more, if you want,"
    quoth he.
" I will have them, my good fellow, but can pay for them," said
    she ;
And she clambered on the wagon, minding not who all were by,
With a laugh of reckless romping in the corner of her eye.

Clinging round his brawny neck, she clasped her fingers white
    and small,
And then whispered, " Quick ! the letters ! thrust them under-
    neath my shawl !
Carry back again *this* package, and be sure that you are spry ! "
And she sweetly smiled upon him from the corner of her eye.

Loud the motley crowd were laughing at the strange, ungirlish
    freak,
And the boy was scared and panting, and so dashed he could not
    speak ;
And, " Miss, *I* have good apples," a bolder lad did cry ;
But she answered, " No, I thank you," from the corner of her
    eye.

With the news of loved ones absent to the dear friends they would
    greet,
Searching them who hungered for them, swift she glided through
    the street.
" There is nothing worth the doing that it does not pay to try,"
Thought the little black-eyed rebel, with a twinkle in her eye.

XXXI

Molly Maguire at Monmouth

THE British army, which had wintered in Philadelphia, evacuated that city on June 18, 1778, and started to march to New York. General Howe, who had been in command, was succeeded by Sir Henry Clinton. As soon as Washington learned of the British movement he started in pursuit, and on Sunday, June 28th, ordered General Charles Lee, who commanded the advance guard, to attack the British left wing near Monmouth Court-House in New Jersey. Lee chose to disregard Washington's orders, and instead of attacking ordered his men to withdraw. Surprised at these tactics the Americans were thrown into disorder, when Washington himself, who had been hurriedly sent for by General Lafayette, dashed up to the advance guard, and, white with anger at Lee's lack of courage or judgment, ordered him to the rear. Washington then took command, re-formed the scattered troops, and, although the British had secured a much more favorable position, succeeded in driving them back. The battle was ended by night, and Clinton managed to get his army away under cover of the darkness.

Washington's rebuke to Lee was one of the incidents that made the battle memorable. But equally historic was the story of Molly Maguire or Molly Pitcher. This woman was a sturdy, red-haired, freckle-faced Irish woman, who had accompanied her husband, a cannonier, on the march. During the battle she carried water to him as he served his cannon. In the thick of the fighting he was killed at his post by a bullet. Molly seized the rammer as it fell from his hand, and sprang to his place by the gun. She stood to her post, and handled the cannon as skilfully as any of the regular cannoniers. The story of her bravery spread through the American ranks, and on the morning after the battle General Washington sent for her, and gave her a commision as sergeant in the Continental Army.

She is usually known as Molly Pitcher, but William Collins chose to call her Molly Maguire.

MOLLY MAGUIRE AT MONMOUTH
By William Collins

On the bloody field of Monmouth
  Flashed the guns of Greene and Wayne.
Fiercely roared the tide of battle,
  Thick the sward was heaped with slain.
Foremost, facing death and danger,
  Hessian, horse, and grenadier,
In the vanguard, fiercely fighting,
  Stood an Irish Cannonier.

Loudly roared his iron cannon,
  Mingling ever in the strife,
And beside him, firm and daring,
  Stood his faithful Irish wife.
Of her bold contempt of danger
  Greene and Lee's Brigades could tell,
Every one knew "Captain Molly,"
  And the army loved her well.

Mollie Pitcher at the Battle of Monmouth

Surged the roar of battle round them,
    Swiftly flew the iron hail,
Forward dashed a thousand bayonets,
    That lone battery to assail.
From the foeman's foremost columns
    Swept a furious fusillade,
Mowing down the massed battalions
    In the ranks of Greene's Brigade.

Fast and faster worked the gunner,
    Soiled with powder, blood, and dust,
English bayonets shone before him,
    Shot and shell around him burst;
Still he fought with reckless daring,
    Stood and manned her long and well,
Till at last the gallant fellow
    Dead—beside his cannon fell.

With a bitter cry of sorrow,
    And a dark and angry frown,
Looked that band of gallant patriots
    At their gunner stricken down.
"Fall back, comrades, it is folly
    Thus to strive against the foe."
"No! not so," cried Irish Molly;
    "We can strike another blow."

*   *   *   *   *

Quickly leaped she to the cannon,
    In her fallen husband's place,
Sponged and rammed it fast and steady,
    Fired it in the foeman's face.
Flashed another ringing volley,
    Roared another from the gun;
"Boys, hurrah!" cried gallant Molly,
    "For the flag of Washington."

Greene's Brigade, though shorn and shattered,
  Slain and bleeding half their men,
When they heard that Irish slogan,
  Turned and charged the foe again.
Knox and Wayne and Morgan rally,
  To the front they forward wheel,
And before their rushing onset
  Clinton's English columns reel.

Still the cannon's voice in anger
  Rolled and rattled o'er the plain,
Till there lay in swarms around it
  Mangled heaps of Hessian slain.
"Forward ! charge them with the bayonet !"
  'Twas the voice of Washington,
And there burst a fiery greeting
  From the Irish woman's gun.

Monckton falls ; against his columns
  Leap the troops of Wayne and Lee,
And before their reeking bayonets
  Clinton's red battalions flee.
Morgan's rifles, fiercely flashing,
  Thin the foe's retreating ranks,
And behind them onward dashing
  Ogden hovers on their flanks.

Fast they fly, these boasting Britons,
  Who in all their glory came,
With their brutal Hessian hirelings
  To wipe out our country's name.
Proudly floats the starry banner,
  Monmouth's glorious field is won,
And in triumph Irish Molly
  Stands beside her smoking gun.

XXXII

Song of Marion's Men

THE British had succeeded in defeating most of the American troops in South Carolina by 1780, and had laid waste much of that state, confiscating plantations, burning houses, and hanging such as they termed traitors without giving them any form of trial. The city of Charleston surrendered to Sir Henry Clinton, the American General Gates was defeated at the battle of Camden, August 16, 1780, and General Sumter at Fishing Creek August 18, 1780. After that there was only one organized American force in South Carolina, "Marion's Brigade," as it was called. This was a band of troopers led by General Francis Marion, a native of South Carolina, whose ancestors were Huguenot refugees. At first his troop contained only twenty men, but more joined his band, and for three years they carried on irregular warfare, harassing the British forces more than regular soldiers could have done.

Marion's men defeated a large body of Tories at Briton's Neck without losing a single man, and soon after beat the enemy twice by sudden attacks when the Tories were unaware of armed men being near. Marion managed to escape General Tarleton by disappearing into a swamp after a chase of twenty-five miles. This won the daring leader the name of

"Swamp Fox," by which he was known all through the countryside.

After the battle of King's Mountain more recruits joined the band. In December, 1780, Marion tried to capture Georgetown, but failed. His nephew, Gabriel Marion, was taken prisoner, and as soon as his name was learned he was executed. The "Swamp Fox" led his band back to a well-hidden island known as Swan Island, and made many sorties through the everglades and forests. Again and again he attacked the British along the Santee and Pedee Rivers. He was never cruel to prisoners, and won a high name for his leadership as well as for his own bravery.

Marion's men succeeded in capturing Georgetown on their third attempt, and fought in the battle of Eutaw Springs, September 8, 1781, which practically ended the British occupation of that part of the new United States of America.

Marion has always been one of the most popular heroes of the Revolution, and the "Swamp Fox" well deserved his fame. He was a gallant leader, and the British and Tories admitted that, although he fought them by stealth, he was never a treacherous foe.

SONG OF MARION'S MEN
By William Cullen Bryant

Our band is few, but true and tried,
  Our leader frank and bold ;
The British soldier trembles
  When Marion's name is told.

MARION AND HIS MEN

Our fortress is the good greenwood,
   Our tent the cypress-tree ;
We know the forest round us,
   As seamen know the sea ;
We know its walks of thorny vines,
   Its glades of reedy grass,
Its safe and silent islands
   Within the dark morass.

Woe to the English soldiery
   That little dread us near !
On them shall light at midnight
   A strange and sudden fear ;
When, waking to their tents on fire,
   They grasp their arms in vain,
And they who stand to face us
   Are beat to earth again ;
And they who fly in terror deem
   A mighty host behind,
And hear the tramp of thousands
   Upon the hollow wind.

Then sweet the hour that brings release
   From danger and from toil ;
We talk the battle over,
   And share the battle's spoil.
The woodland rings with laugh and shout,
   As if a hunt were up,
And woodland flowers are gathered
   To crown the soldier's cup.
With merry songs we mock the wind
   That in the pine-top grieves,
And slumber long and sweetly
   On beds of oaken leaves.

Well knows the fair and friendly moon
  The band that Marion leads —
The glitter of their rifles,
  The scampering of their steeds.
'Tis life to guide the fiery barb
  Across the moonlight plain;
'Tis life to feel the night-wind
  That lifts his tossing mane.
A moment in the British camp —
  A moment — and away,
Back to the pathless forest,
  Before the peep of day.

Grave men there are by broad Santee,
  Grave men with hoary hairs;
Their hearts are all with Marion,
  For Marion are their prayers.
And lovely ladies greet our band,
  With kindest welcoming,
With smiles like those of summer,
  And tears like those of spring.
For them we wear these trusty arms,
  And lay them down no more
Till we have driven the Briton,
  Forever, from our shore.

XXXIII

Hail Columbia

IN 1798 the United States Congress authorized the enrollment of an army of ten thousand men, and instructed the President to order the captains of all American war-ships to seize any armed French vessels that were found hovering near the coast and attacking American merchantmen. Patriotic feeling ran high, and Joseph Hopkinson of Philadelphia wrote this poem to express the feelings of the times.

This letter from Joseph Hopkinson is given in " Poets and Poetry of America," edited by Rev. R. W. Griswold. " It [Hail Columbia] was written in the summer of 1798, when war with France was thought to be inevitable. Congress was then in session in Philadelphia, deliberating upon that important subject, and acts of hostility had actually taken place. The contest between England and France was raging, and the people of the United States were divided into parties for the one side or the other, some thinking that policy and duty required us to espouse the cause of republican France, as she was called ; while others were for connecting ourselves with England, under the belief that she was the great conservative power of good principles and safe government. The violation of our rights by both belligerents was forcing us from the just and wise policy of President Washington, which was to do equal justice to both, to take part with neither, but to preserve a strict and honest neutrality between them. The prospect of a rupture with France was exceedingly offensive to that portion of the people who espoused her cause, and the violence of the spirit of party has never risen higher, I think not so high, in our country, as it did at that time, upon that question. The theatre was then open in our city. A young man belonging to it, whose talent was as a singer, was about to take his benefit. I had known him when he was at school. On this acquaintance, he called on me one Saturday afternoon, his benefit being announced for the following Monday. His prospects were very disheartening ; but he said that if he could get a patriotic song adapted to the tune of the 'President's March,' he did not doubt of a full house; that the poets of the theatrical corps had been trying to accomplish it, but had not succeeded. I told him I would try what I could do for him. The object of the author was to get up an *American spirit*, which should be independent of and above the interests, passions, and policy of both belligerents : and look and feel exclusively for our own honor and rights. No allusion is made to France or England, or the quarrel between them : or to the question, which was the most at fault in their treatment of us : of course the song found favor with both parties, for both were Americans ; at least neither could disavow the sentiments and feelings it inculcated."

The song was first sung at the Chestnut Street Theatre in Philadelphia, in May, 1798 ; and became tremendously popular.

The air to which it was sung was one written by Phyla, a naturalized German, living in Philadelphia, an air which had been used at the inauguration of Washington, and was known as "The President's March."

HAIL COLUMBIA
By Joseph Hopkinson

Hail! Columbia, happy land!
Hail! ye heroes, heav'n-born band,
Who fought and bled in freedom's cause,
Who fought and bled in freedom's cause,
And when the storm of war was gone,
Enjoyed the peace your valor won;
Let independence be your boast,
Ever mindful what it cost,
Ever grateful for the prize,
Let its altar reach the skies;
    Firm, united let us be,
    Rallying round our liberty,
    As a band of brothers joined,
    Peace and safety we shall find.

Immortal patriots, rise once more!
Defend your rights, defend your shore;
Let no rude foe with impious hand,
Let no rude foe with impious hand,
Invade the shrine where sacred lies
Of toil and blood the well-earned prize;
While offering peace, sincere and just,
In Heav'n we place a manly trust,
That truth and justice may prevail,
And every scheme of bondage fail.

Sound, sound the trump of fame !
Let Washington's great name
Ring through the world with loud applause !
Ring through the world with loud applause !
Let every clime to freedom dear
Listen with a joyful ear ;
With equal skill, with steady pow'r,
He governs in the fearful hour
Of horrid war, or guides with ease
The happier time of honest peace.

Behold the chief, who now commands,
Once more to serve his country stands,
The rock on which the storm will beat !
The rock on which the storm will beat !
But armed in virtue, firm and true,
His hopes are fixed on Heav'n and you.
When hope was sinking in dismay,
When gloom obscured Columbia's day,
His steady mind, from changes free,
Resolved on death or liberty.

 Firm, united let us be,
 Rallying round our liberty,
 As a band of brothers joined,
 Peace and safety we shall find.

XXXIV

Casabianca

THE story of this brave boy has become famous through Mrs. Hemans' poem, but, although the incidents related in it have been ascribed to a number of battles at sea, there is no historical proof that such a boy took part in any of them. Usually, however, he is spoken of as the ten-year-old son of Admiral Brueys, commander of the French man-of-war *L' Orient*.

This ship was engaged in the battle of the Nile fought between Napoleon and the English on August 1, 1798. Nelson was in command of the English fleet, and won one of his greatest victories. During the battle the French Admiral Brueys was mortally wounded, and was left on the deck of his ship. As night came on the ship was seen to be on fire, and Nelson ordered his men to board her and rescue the officers and crew. All the Frenchmen left except the boy Casabianca, who refused to go, saying that his father had told him not to leave the ship, and that he could not disobey that order.

The man-of-war was in danger of blowing up at any minute, and the English sailors had to put off in their boats. They had barely time to pull away before the flames reached the powder and the ship exploded.

Although it cannot be said positively that Casabianca

was the boy of the battle of the Nile facts **seem to** prove that a boy did **such an** act at that battle.

CASABIANCA

By Felicia Dorothea Hemans

The boy stood on the burning deck
    Whence all but him had fled ;
The flame that lit the battle's wreck
    Shone round him o'er the dead.

Yet beautiful and bright he stood,
    As born to rule the storm ;
A creature of heroic blood,
    A proud, though childlike form.

The flames rolled on—he would not go
    Without his father's word ;
That father, faint in death below,
    His voice no longer heard.

He called aloud—" Say, father, say,
    If yet my task is done ? "
He knew not that the chieftain lay
    Unconscious of his son.

" Speak, father ! " once again he cried,
    " If I may yet be gone ! "
And but the booming shots replied,
    And fast the flames rolled on.

Upon his brow he felt their breath,
    And in his waving hair,
And looked from that lone post of death
    In still, yet brave despair.

And shouted but once more aloud,
  " My father ! must I stay ? "
While o'er him fast, through sail and shroud,
  The wreathing fires made way.

They wrapt the ship in splendor wild,
  They caught the flag on high,
And streamed above the gallant child,
  Like banners in the sky.

There came a burst of thunder sound—
  The boy—oh ! where was he ?
Ask of the winds that far around
  With fragments strewed the sea ! —

With mast, and helm, and pennon fair
  That well had borne their part—
But the noblest thing that perished there
  Was that young, faithful heart.

XXXV

Hohenlinden

THE little village of Hohenlinden, or Linden, as it was often called, stands in a pine forest of Upper Bavaria, on the banks of the swift-flowing river Iser, about twenty miles distant from Munich. In December, 1800, two great armies, the one Austrian, the other French and Bavarian, commanded by Napoleon's General Moreau, drew close to each other along the river. Snow had been falling for several days. The weather was bitterly cold. The armies opened fire, however, and a great battle was fought in the forest, although the snow-storm was so blinding that the soldiers could only distinguish their enemies by the flash of their guns. The battle raged through the woods, across the hills, and along the river. The French and Bavarians finally won, and the Emperor of Austria had to accept Napoleon's terms of peace in order to save his capital of Vienna from capture. In the poem "Frank" means the French, "Hun" stands for the Austrians, and "Munich" refers to the Bavarians and their capital.

During his travels in Germany the English poet Campbell saw a battle from a convent near Ratisbon, and he also visited the field of Ingolstadt after a battle. From these experiences he wrote his poem on Hohenlinden.

HOHENLINDEN
By Thomas Campbell

On Linden when the sun was low,
All bloodless lay the untrodden snow,
And dark as winter was the flow
Of Iser, rolling rapidly.

But Linden saw another sight
When the drum beat, at dead of night,
Commanding fires of death to light
The darkness of her scenery.

By torch and trumpet fast arrayed
Each horseman drew his battle blade,
And furious every charger neighed,
To join the dreadful revelry.

Then shook the hills with thunder riven,
Then rushed the steed to battle driven,
And louder than the bolts of heaven
Far flashed the red artillery.

And redder yet those fires shall glow
On Linden's hills of blood-stained snow,
And darker yet shall be the flow
Of Iser, rolling rapidly.

'Tis morn, but scarce yon lurid sun
Can pierce the war-clouds, rolling dun,
Where furious Frank and fiery Hun
Shout in their sulphurous canopy.

The combat deepens.   On, ye brave,
Who rush to glory, or the grave !
Wave, Munich, all thy banners wave !
And charge with all thy chivalry !

Ah ! few shall part where many meet !
The snow shall be their winding-sheet,
And every turf beneath their feet
Shall be a soldier's sepulchre.

XXXVI

Battle of the Baltic

AT the time when Napoleon I was Emperor of the French England was practically the only country that could hold its own against him, and this was chiefly due to the victories won by the British navy under Lord Nelson. During the long contest with France the government of England claimed the right to search all neutral ships, for the purpose of preventing secret trade with France. This claim was resisted by several other nations, and in 1800 Russia, Sweden, Prussia, and Denmark formed an alliance known as the " Second Armed Neutrality," for the purpose of opposing the claim.

The English sent a fleet of fifty-two ships to the Baltic to break up the alliance. Horatio Nelson was second in command. He was assigned the attack when, on March 30, 1801, his advance squadron of thirty-six vessels entered the Danish harbor of Copenhagen. The British commander, Sir Hyde Parker, gave the signal to cease firing after the battle had raged for three hours. Nelson saw the signal, but placing his spy-glass to his blind eye, said to his lieutenants, " I really don't see the signal. Keep mine for closer battle still flying. That's the way I answer such signals. Nail mine to the mast." The battle lasted for five hours, and ended in complete victory for the English fleet. As a reward for his skill in this battle, which Nelson declared was the most terrible in which he had ever taken part, he was made a viscount and given the thanks of the English Parliament.

BATTLE OF THE BALTIC

By Thomas Campbell

Of Nelson and the north
   Sing the glorious day's renown,
When to battle fierce came forth
   All the might of Denmark's crown,
And her arms along the deep proudly shone ;
   By each gun the lighted brand
   In a bold, determined hand,
   And the prince of all the land
Led them on.

Like leviathans afloat
   Lay their bulwarks on the brine ;
While the sign of battle flew
   On the lofty British line —
It was ten of April morn by the chime.
   As they drifted on their path
   There was silence deep as death ;
   And the boldest held his breath
For a time.

But the might of England flushed
   To anticipate the scene ;
And her van the fleeter rushed
   O'er the deadly space between.

" Hearts of oak ! " our captain cried ; when each gun
　　From its adamantine lips
　　Spread a death-shade round the ships,
　　Like the hurricane eclipse
Of the sun.

Again ! again ! again !
　　And the havoc did not slack,
Till a feeble cheer the Dane
　　To our cheering sent us back ;
Their shots along the deep slowly boom —
　　Then ceased — and all is wail,
　　As they strike the shattered sail,
　　Or in conflagration pale,
Light the gloom.

Out spoke the victor then,
　　As he hailed them o'er the wave :
" Ye are brothers ! ye are men !
　　And we conquer but to save ;
So peace instead of death let us bring ;
　　But yield, proud foe, thy fleet,
　　With the crews, at England's feet,
　　And make submission meet
To our king."

Then Denmark blessed our chief,
　　That he gave her wounds repose ;
And the sounds of joy and grief
　　From her people wildly rose,
As death withdrew his shades from the day.
　　While the sun looked smiling bright
　　O'er a wide and woeful sight,
　　Where the fires of funeral light
Died away.

Now joy, old England, raise !
  For the tidings of thy might,
By the festal cities' blaze,
  Whilst the wine-cup shines in light ;
And yet, amidst that joy and uproar,
  Let us think of them that sleep
  Full many a fathom deep,
  By thy wild and stormy steep,
Elsinore !

Brave hearts ! to Britain's pride
  Once so faithful and so true,
On the deck of fame that died,
  With the gallant, good Riou —
Soft sigh the winds of heaven o'er their grave !
  While the billow mournful rolls,
  And the mermaid's song condoles,
  Singing glory to the souls
Of the brave !

XXXVII

An Incident of the French Camp

THE old city of Ratisbon, which is called Regensburg in German, is situated on the river Danube, in Bavaria. It had been besieged no less than sixteen times since the tenth century when Napoleon, Emperor of the French, attacked it in 1809. Napoleon was at that time waging a victorious campaign against Austria, and had stopped at Ratisbon on his march to Vienna, the Austrian capital. The Austrians defended the city, and Napoleon ordered a bombardment, which destroyed some two hundred houses and a large part of the suburbs.

The poem tells how as Napoleon stood in his favorite attitude, head thrust forward, legs wide apart, arms locked behind his back, watching the attack, and possibly wondering what would happen if his general, Marshal Lannes, should waver, a rider dashed up to him. The rider, a boy, flung himself from his horse, and reported that the French had taken the city, that he had planted the Emperor's eagle flag on the walls, and had ridden back a mile or more to tell him.

Napoleon's eye flashed, then softened as he looked at the brave boy. "You're wounded!" he said. "Nay, I'm killed, sire," the boy answered, and fell dead beside him.

The incident is generally regarded as true, but the hero is said to have been a man, instead of a boy, as in Browning's version of it.

AN INCIDENT OF THE FRENCH CAMP
By Robert Browning

You know we French stormed Ratisbon :
  A mile or so away,
On a little mound, Napoleon
  Stood on our storming-day ;
With neck out-thrust, you fancy how,
  Legs wide, arms locked behind,
As if to balance the prone brow,
  Oppressive with its mind.

Just as perhaps he mused, " My plans
  That soar, to earth may fall,
Let once my army-leader Lannes
  Waver at yonder wall,"—
Out 'twixt the battery-smokes there flew
  A rider, bound on bound
Full-galloping ; nor bridle drew
  Until he reached the mound.

Then off there flung in smiling joy,
  And held himself erect
By just his horse's mane, a boy :
  You hardly could suspect —
(So tight he kept his lips compressed,
  Scarce any blood came through)
You looked twice ere you saw his breast
  Was all but shot in two.

" Well," cried he, " Emperor, by God's grace
 We've got you Ratisbon !
The marshal's in the market-place,
 And you'll be there anon
To see your flag-bird flap his vans
 Where I, to heart's desire,
Perched him ! " The chief's eye flashed ; his plans
 Soared up again like fire.

The chief's eye flashed ; but presently
 Softened itself, as sheathes
A film the mother eagle's eye
 When her bruised eaglet breathes ;
" You're wounded ! " " Nay," his soldier's pride
 Touched to the quick, he said :
" I'm killed, sire ! " And, his chief beside,
 Smiling, the boy fell dead.

XXXVIII

The Star-Spangled Banner

DURING the War of 1812 between the United States and England the British fleet, under Admiral Sir George Cockborn, on September 13, 1814, began the bombardment of Fort McHenry, which was situated two miles above Baltimore. The English forces had captured several Americans at a place called Marlborough and were detaining them, although some were civilians. A gentleman of Baltimore, Francis Scott Key by name, set out with a flag of truce to try to secure the release of one of these civilians, who was a friend of his. He reached the mouth of the Patuxent when he was captured. The British feared to let him return to Baltimore lest he should disclose their plans for taking the city, and so Key was brought up Chesapeake Bay and put on board the admiral's flag-ship.

The English officers on the ship were confident that Fort McHenry would surrender and Baltimore be easily captured, and Key had to listen to their predictions and watch the bombardment all day. The American flag was still flying from the fort when night prevented his watching it longer. The bombardment continued all night, but at dawn on September 14th Key saw that the flag still bade defiance to the fleet. At a white-heat of emotion Key then and there wrote the lines of " **The**

Star-Spangled Banner," one of the most stirring of all American songs.

The first copy of the song was written on the British flag-ship while the guns were thundering. As soon as he was released Key hurried back to Baltimore and there corrected what he had written. He then took it to a printer, who struck it off as a broadside, or poem printed on a large sheet of paper. As soon as it appeared it created enthusiasm and sprang into quick fame. The air to which it was sung was selected from a volume of music for the flute, and was called "Anacreon in Heaven," an English glee composed by Samuel Arnold. This air had already been used for the American patriotic song called "Adams and Liberty." It suited the words of Key's poem well, and soon became inseparably connected with the "Star-Spangled Banner."

THE STAR-SPANGLED BANNER
By Francis Scott Key

O say, can you see, by the dawn's early light,
    What so proudly we hailed at the twilight's last gleaming?
Whose broad stripes and bright stars through the perilous fight
    O'er the ramparts we watched were so gallantly streaming!
And the rockets' red glare, the bombs bursting in air,
Gave proof through the night that our flag was still there;
    Oh, say, does that star-spangled banner yet wave
    O'er the land of the free and the home of the brave?

On the shore, dimly seen through the mists of the deep,
    Where the foe's haughty host in dread silence reposes,
What is that which the breeze o'er the towering steep,
    As it fitfully blows, now conceals, now discloses?

Now it catches the gleam of the morning's first beam,
In full glory reflected, now shines on the stream ;
   'Tis the star-spangled banner !　O long may it wave
   O'er the land of the free and the home of the brave !

And where is that band who so vauntingly swore
   That the havoc of war and the battle's confusion,
A home and a country should leave us no more ?
   Their blood has washed out their foul footsteps' pollution.
No refuge could save the hireling and slave,
From terror of flight, or the gloom of the grave :
   And the star-spangled banner in triumph doth wave
   O'er the land of the free and the home of the brave !

Oh ! thus be it ever, when freemen shall stand
   Between their loved homes and the war's desolation !
Blest with victory and peace, may the heaven-rescued land
   Praise the Power that made and preserved us a nation !
Then conquer we must, for our cause it is just,
And this be our motto :—" In God is our trust ! "
   And the star-spangled banner in triumph shall wave
   O'er the land of the free and the home of the brave.

XXXIX

The Battle of New Orleans

At the same time that British armies were attacking Washington and Baltimore and a British squadron fighting that of Commodore Perry on Lake Erie in the War of 1812, England was fitting out a secret expedition to sail from Jamaica and land in Louisiana. Fifty British ships carried 7,000 British soldiers across the Gulf of Mexico to the channel near the entrance of Lake Borgne, approaching the small city of New Orleans midway between the Mississippi River and Mobile Bay. The fleet anchored here, and easily defeating a few American gunboats, landed their army on an island at the mouth of the Pearl River. They intended to march on New Orleans and capture it by surprise.

Andrew Jackson, a major-general in the American army, had been sent to defend the South from invasion. He reached New Orleans early in December, 1814, and at once began to recruit volunteers. All who would fight the enemy were welcomed to his camp, free negroes were enrolled, convicts were released to become soldiers, the lieutenants of a freebooter named Jean Lafitte, who had made his headquarters at Barataria, and many of his men who had been captured, were freed to join the army. Jackson strengthened the forts of the city and made every preparation to receive the enemy. Five thousand effective fighting men were soon under his command, less than one thousand of whom were soldiers in the regular army.

When the British finally appeared, it was they, and not the Americans, who were surprised. Jackson attacked them as soon as they were in sight, December 23, 1814, and checked their advance. He then entrenched his little force opposite the British, and had them well sheltered by the time the enemy had prepared to give battle. Meantime the British general, Pakenham, had been waiting for larger cannon and reinforcements.

On January 8, 1815, the British advanced, planning to carry the American lines by storm. The British had 10,000 veteran troops, the Americans less than half that number, and most of these raw backwoodsmen. But Jackson's men were born to the use of the rifle, and their firing was wonderfully steady and accurate. The British had to advance over a wide, bare plain, and the American batteries ploughed through their ranks, while the riflemen met them with a raking fire. The veteran English fought with the utmost bravery, the Highlanders flung themselves again and again at the entrenchments, and soldiers who had fought under Wellington in Spain and with Pakenham at Salamanca charged at the blazing line. Pakenham and many of his highest officers were killed, and the British army was finally forced into retreat. They had lost over two thousand men, while the Americans were reported to have lost eight killed and thirteen wounded.

The Battle of New Orleans

It was an overwhelming victory for Andrew Jackson and his volunteers.

The British returned to their ships and sailed away. Neither side knew that a treaty of peace had been signed at Ghent in Brussels two weeks earlier, and that the battle of New Orleans had been fought after the war had ended.

The story of the battle is supposed to be told in this poem by one of the settlers who marched to New Orleans with William Carroll, major-general of the Tennessee militia.

THE BATTLE OF NEW ORLEANS
By Thomas Dunn English
(From " The Boys' Book of Battle Lyrics.")

Here, in my rude log cabin,
    Few poorer men there be
Among the mountain ranges
    Of Eastern Tennessee.
My limbs are weak and shrunken,
    White hairs upon my brow,
My dog—lie still, old fellow !—
    My sole companion now.
Yet I, when young and lusty,
    Have gone through stirring scenes,
For I went down with Carroll
    To fight at New Orleans.

You say you'd like to hear me
    The stirring story tell
Of those who stood the battle
    And those who fighting fell.

Short work to count our losses —
  We stood and dropp'd the foe
As easily as by firelight
  Men shoot the buck or doe.
And while they fell by hundreds
  Upon the bloody plain,
Of us, fourteen were wounded,
  And only eight were slain.

The eighth of January,
  Before the break of day,
Our raw and hasty levies
  Were brought into array.
No cotton-bales before us —
  Some fool that falsehood told;
Before us was an earthwork,
  Built from the swampy mold.
And there we stood in silence,
  And waited with a frown,
To greet with bloody welcome
  The bulldogs of the Crown.

The heavy fog of morning
  Still hid the plain from sight,
When came a thread of scarlet
  Marked faintly in the white.
We fired a single cannon,
  And as its thunders roll'd
The mist before us lifted
  In many a heavy fold.
The mist before us lifted,
  And in their bravery fine
Came rushing to their ruin
  The fearless British line.

Then from our waiting cannons
  Leap'd forth the deadly flame,
To meet the advancing columns
  That swift and steady came.
The thirty-twos of Crowley
  And Bluchi's twenty-four,
To Spotts's eighteen-pounders
  Responded with their roar,
Sending the grape-shot deadly
  That marked its pathway plain,
And paved the road it travel'd
  With corpses of the slain.

Our rifles firmly grasping,
  And heedless of the din,
We stood in silence waiting
  For orders to begin.
Our fingers on the triggers,
  Our hearts, with anger stirr'd,
Grew still more fierce and eager
  As Jackson's voice was heard :
"Stand steady !   Waste no powder ;
  Wait till your shots will tell !
To-day the work you finish —
  See that you do it well ! "

Their columns drawing nearer,
  We felt our patience tire,
When came the voice of Carroll,
  Distinct and measured, "Fire ! "
Oh ! then you should have mark'd us
  Our volleys on them pour —
Have heard our joyous rifles
  Ring sharply through the roar,

And seen their foremost columns
  Melt hastily away
As snow in mountain gorges
  Before the floods of May.

They soon reform'd their columns,
  And 'mid the fatal rain
We never ceased to hurtle
  Came to their work again.
The Forty-fourth is with them,
  That first its laurels won
With stout old Abercrombie
  Beneath an eastern sun.
It rushes to the battle,
  And, though within the rear
Its leader is a laggard,
  It shows no signs of fear.

It did not need its colonel,
  For soon there came instead
An eagle-eyed commander,
  And on its march he led.
'Twas Pakenham, in person,
  The leader of the field ;
I knew it by the cheering
  That loudly round him peal'd ;
And by his quick, sharp movement,
  We felt his heart was stirr'd,
As when at Salamanca,
  He led the fighting Third.

I raised my rifle quickly,
  I sighted at his breast,
God save the gallant leader
  And take him to his rest !

I did not draw the trigger,
   I could not for my life.
So calm he sat his charger
   Amid the deadly strife,
That in my fiercest moment
   A prayer arose from me,—
God save that gallant leader,
   Our foeman though he be.

Sir Edward's charger staggers:
   He leaps at once to ground,
And ere the beast falls bleeding
   Another horse is found.
His right arm falls—'tis wounded;
   He waves on high his left;
In vain he leads the movement,
   The ranks in twain are cleft.
The men in scarlet waver
   Before the men in brown,
And fly in utter panic —
   The soldiers of the Crown !

I thought the work was over,
   But nearer shouts were heard,
And came, with Gibbs to head it,
   The gallant Ninety-third.
Then Pakenham, exulting,
   With proud and joyous glance,
Cried, " Children of the tartan—
   Bold Highlanders—advance.
Advance to scale the breastworks
   And drive them from their hold,
And show the stanchless courage
   That mark'd your sires of old ! "

His voice as yet was ringing,
　　When, quick as light, there came
The roaring of a cannon,
　　And earth seemed all aflame.
Who causes thus the thunder
　　The doom of men to speak?
It is the Baritarian,
　　The fearless Dominique.
Down through the marshall'd Scotsmen
　　The step of death is heard,
And by the fierce tornado
　　Falls half the Ninety-third.

The smoke passed slowly upward,
　　And, as it soared on high,
I saw the brave commander
　　In dying anguish lie.
They bear him from the battle
　　Who never fled the foe;
Unmoved by death around them
　　His bearers softly go.
In vain their care, so gentle,
　　Fades earth and all its scenes;
The man of Salamanca
　　Lies dead at New Orleans.

But where were his lieutenants?
　　Had they in terror fled?
No! Keane was sorely wounded
　　And Gibbs as good as dead.
Brave Wilkinson commanding,
　　A major of brigade,
The shatter'd force to rally,
　　A final effort made.

He led it up our ramparts,
  Small glory did he gain —
Our captives some, while others fled,
  And he himself was slain.

The stormers had retreated,
  The bloody work was o'er;
The feet of the invaders
  Were seen to leave our shore.
We rested on our rifles
  And talk'd about the fight,
When came a sudden murmur
  Like fire from left to right;
We turned and saw our chieftain,
  And then, good friend of mine,
You should have heard the cheering
  That ran along the line.

For well our men remembered
  How little, when they came,
Had they but native courage,
  And trust in Jackson's name;
How through the day he labored,
  How kept the vigils still,
Till discipline controlled us,
  A stronger power than will;
And how he hurled us at them
  Within the evening hour,
That red night in December,
  And made us feel our power.

In answer to our shouting
  Fire lit his eye of gray;
Erect, but thin and pallid,
  He passed upon his bay.

Weak from the baffled fever,
　And shrunken in each limb,
The swamps of Alabama
　Had done their work on him.
But spite of that and fasting,
　And hours of sleepless care,
The soul of Andrew Jackson
　Shone forth in glory there.

XL

The Eve of Waterloo

THIS is a part of one of Byron's finest poems, "Childe Harold." It relates the events of the night before the battle of Quatre Bras, which was fought near Brussels, the capital of Belgium, on June 16, 1815, and was the preliminary of the great battle of Waterloo, fought two days later.

Three nights before the battle of Waterloo the English Duchess of Richmond gave a ball in Brussels, and invited many of the officers of the allied English and Prussian armies, which were at war with the French. The Duke of Wellington, commander-in-chief of the English army, was said to have been one of the guests. While the ball was at its height a messenger brought word to Wellington that the French under Napoleon were advancing towards the city. He did not wish to alarm the people, and so kept the information secret, but he sent the officers one by one to their regiments, and finally left for the field himself.

In the poem, however, the dancers at the ball heard a distant booming. At first they paid little heed to it, and went on with the dancing ; but presently the sound grew louder and clearer, and they recognized it as the roar of cannon. The first to hear it was Frederick

William, Duke of Brunswick, whose father had been killed in battle. He left for the front at once, and was killed the next day, June 16th, in the battle of Quatre Bras.

The officers said farewell to the ladies, and hurried from the ball to mount and ride against the French; while the frightened citizens crowded the streets, fearing that Napoleon was about to enter Brussels.

Waterloo was a great victory for the English and Prussian armies. It was the real end of Napoleon's all-conquering career, and led to his capture and banishment to the island of St. Helena.

THE EVE OF WATERLOO

By George Gordon Noel, Lord Byron

There was a sound of revelry by night,
　And Belgium's capital had gathered then
Her beauty and her chivalry, and bright
　The lamps shone o'er fair women and brave men.
A thousand hearts beat happily; and when
　Music arose with its voluptuous swell,
Soft eyes looked love to eyes which spake again,
　And all went merry as a marriage bell;
　But hush! hark! a deep sound strikes like a rising
　　knell!

Did ye not hear it?—No; 'twas but the wind,
　Or the car rattling o'er the stony street;
On with the dance! let joy be unconfined;
　No sleep till morn, when youth and pleasure meet
　To chase the glowing hours with flying feet.

But hark !—that heavy sound breaks in once more,
  As if the clouds its echo would repeat ;
And nearer, clearer, deadlier than before ;
Arm ! arm ! it is—it is—the cannon's opening roar !

Within a windowed niche of that high hall
  Sate Brunswick's fated chieftain ; he did hear
That sound the first amidst the festival,
  And caught its tone with death's prophetic ear ;
  And when they smiled because he deemed it near,
His heart more truly knew that peal too well
  Which stretched his father on a bloody bier,
And roused the vengeance blood alone could quell ;
He rushed into the field, and, foremost fighting, fell.

Ah ! then and there was hurrying to and fro,
  And gathering tears, and tremblings of distress,
And cheeks all pale, which, but an hour ago,
  Blushed at the praise of their own loveliness.
  And there were sudden partings, such as press
The life from out young hearts, and choking sighs
  Which ne'er might be repeated ; who would guess
If ever more should meet those mutual eyes,
Since upon night so sweet such awful morn could rise !

And there was mounting in hot haste ; the steed,
  The mustering squadron, and the clattering car,
Went pouring forward with impetuous speed,
  And swiftly forming in the ranks of war ;
  And the deep thunder, peal on peal afar ;
And near, the beat of the alarming drum
  Roused up the soldier ere the morning star ;
While thronged the citizens with terror dumb,
Or whispering, with white lips—" The foe ! they come !
    they come ! "

XLI

Marco Bozzaris

AT the beginning of the nineteenth century Greece, which had once been one of the greatest countries in the world, was subject to the rule of her powerful neighbor, Turkey. But in 1821 the fire of patriotism was rekindled, and the Greeks began a war of independence. One of the most heroic of the Greek leaders was Marco Bozzaris. He was in command of a small band of his countrymen, and planned to surprise a much larger Turkish force after nightfall. In this poem, written by Fitz-Greene Halleck, an American author, the story of the attack is told.

The Turkish commander and his men were sleeping in their camps, dreaming of victory over the Greeks, while at the same hour of midnight Marco Bozzaris was making ready his band of Suliotes, or men whose homes were near the Suli mountains and river in the northwestern part of Greece. The Turkish camp was not far distant from Missilonghi, which is near the entrance to the Gulf of Corinth, near the head of which gulf the earlier Greeks, in 479 B. C., had defeated a great invading army of Persians at the battle of Platæa.

Bozzaris attacked the Turks, and small though his band was, they took the enemy so completely by surprise that they won a very decisive victory. But the gallant leader himself was killed. The poem tells how he won glory, and how death is welcomed by the victorious warrior, as was the cry of land to Columbus of Genoa when his lookout caught the fragrance of the palms and groves of Hayti, mistaking them for India. Pilgrims from foreign lands shall seek the home of Bozzaris to hear again the story of his victory and of his country's independence.

His cause was successful, and six years after this battle near Missilonghi Turkey was forced to grant Greece her freedom, and that country, which had been in subjection for almost four centuries, became an independent nation. It was in this war that the poet Byron and other Englishmen who loved the history of ancient Greece and the cause of liberty fought by the side of Marco Bozzaris.

MARCO BOZZARIS

By Fitz-Greene Halleck

At midnight, in his guarded tent,
    The Turk was dreaming of the hour
When Greece, her knee in suppliance bent,
    Should tremble at his power ;
In dreams, through camp and court he bore
The trophies of a conqueror ;
    In dreams, his song of triumph heard ;
Then wore his monarch's signet-ring ;
Then press'd that monarch's throne—a king :
As wild his thoughts, and gay of wing,
    As Eden's garden bird.

At midnight, in the forest shades,
   Bozzaris ranged his Suliote band,
True as the steel of their tried blades,
   Heroes in heart and hand.
There had the Persian's thousands stood,
There had the glad earth drunk their blood,
   On old Platæa's day ;
And now there breathed that haunted air,
The sons of sires who conquer'd there,
With arm to strike, and soul to dare,
   As quick, as far, as they.

An hour pass'd on : the Turk awoke :
   That bright dream was his last.
He woke to hear his sentries shriek,
   " To arms ! they come ! the Greek ! the Greek ! "
He woke, to die 'midst flame and smoke,
And shout, and groan, and sabre-stroke,
   And death-shots falling thick and fast
As lightnings from the mountain cloud,
And heard, with voice as trumpet loud,
   Bozzaris cheer his band :
" Strike !—till the last arm'd foe expires ;
Strike !—for your altars and your fires ;
Strike !—for the green graves of your sires ;
   God, and your native land ! "

They fought like brave men, long and well ;
   They piled that ground with Moslem slain ;
They conquer'd ;—but Bozzaris fell,
   Bleeding at every vein.
His few surviving comrades saw
His smile when rang their loud hurrah,

And the red field was won;
Then saw in death his eyelids close,
Calmly as to a night's repose,—
Like flowers at set of sun.

Come to the bridal chamber, Death,
Come to the mother's, when she feels,
For the first time, her first-born's breath;
Come, when the blessed seals
That close the pestilence are broke,
And crowded cities wail its stroke:
Come in consumption's ghastly form,
The earthquake shock, the ocean storm;
Come when the heart beats high and warm
With banquet song and dance and wine;
And thou art terrible:—the tear,
The groan, the knell, the pall, the bier,
And all we know, or dream, or fear,
Of agony, are thine.

But to the hero, when his sword
Has won the battle for the free,
Thy voice sounds like a prophet's word,
And in its hollow tones are heard
The thanks of millions yet to be.
Come when his task of fame is wrought;
Come, with her laurel-leaf, blood-bought;
Come in her crowning hour,—and then
Thy sunken eye's unearthly light
To him is welcome as the sight
Of sky and stars to prison'd men;
Thy grasp is welcome as the hand
Of brother in a foreign land;

Thy summons welcome as the cry
That told the Indian isles were nigh
  To the world-seeking Genoese,
When the land-wind, from woods of palm,
And orange groves, and fields of balm,
  Blew o'er the Haytien seas.

Bozzaris ! with the storied brave
  Greece nurtured in her glory's time,
Rest thee: there is no prouder grave,
  Even in her own proud clime.
She wore no funeral weeds for thee,
  Nor bade the dark hearse wave its plume,
Like torn branch from death's leafless tree,
In sorrow's pomp and pageantry,
  The heartless luxury of the tomb ;
But she remembers thee as one
  Long loved, and for a season gone ;
For thee her poet's lyre is wreathed,
Her marble wrought, her music breathed ;
For thee she rings the birthday bells ;
Of thee her babes' first lisping tells ;
For thine her evening prayer is said,
At palace couch and cottage bed :
Her soldier, closing with the foe,
Gives for thy sake a deadlier blow ;
His plighted maiden, when she fears
For him, the joy of her young years,
Thinks of thy fate, and checks her tears ;
  And she, the mother of thy boys,
Though in her eye and faded cheek
Is read the grief she will not speak,
  The memory of her buried joys,—
And even she who gave thee birth
Will, by their pilgrim-circled hearth,

Talk of thy doom without a sigh ;
For thou art Freedom's now, and Fame's,
One of the few, th' immortal names
That were not born to die.

XLII

Ye Mariners of England

ENGLAND has always been called "Mistress of the Seas," a title well deserved because of her great sailors. In times of war her safety is usually entrusted to the fleets that guard the North Sea, the Channel, and the Irish coasts. The great strength of the English navy has always served to prevent enemies from landing on her shores, and it was this strength that prevented Napoleon from invading the British Isles at the time when he had overcome every other nation in Europe.

This poem of Thomas Campbell is a call to the English sailors to prove themselves worthy of their great sea-fighters of the past. He names Admiral Blake, who fought and defeated the Dutch and the Spanish navies in the seventeenth century, and Lord Nelson, the great admiral of Napoleon's time. Nelson defeated Napoleon's navy at the battle of the Nile and the battle of Trafalgar. The latter battle was fought in 1805 against the French and Spanish fleets combined, and made England supreme on the sea. At the beginning of the engagement Nelson flew the signal "England expects every man to do his duty." He himself was mortally wounded.

In the last stanza Campbell speaks of "the meteor flag of England," using that simile because of the exceedingly brilliant red of the English ensign.

YE MARINERS OF ENGLAND
By Thomas Campbell

Ye mariners of England,
  That guard our native seas,
Whose flag has braved, a thousand years,
  The battle and the breeze,
Your glorious standard launch again,
  To match another foe !
And sweep through the deep
  While the stormy winds do blow —
While the battle rages loud and long,
  And the stormy winds do blow.

The spirits of your fathers
  Shall start from every wave !
For the deck it was their field of fame,
  And ocean was their grave.
Where Blake and mighty Nelson fell
  Your manly hearts shall glow,
As ye sweep through the deep
  While the stormy winds do blow —
While the battle rages loud and long,
  And the stormy winds do blow.

Britannia needs no bulwarks,
  No towers along the steep ;
Her march is o'er the mountain-wave,
  Her home is on the deep.
With thunders from her native oak
  She quells the floods below,
As they roar on the shore
  When the stormy winds do blow —
When the battle rages loud and long,
  And the stormy winds do blow.

The meteor flag of England
  Shall yet terrific burn,
Till danger's troubled night depart,
  And the star of peace return.
Then, then, ye ocean-warriors !
  Our song and feast shall flow
To the fame of your name,
  When the storm has ceased to blow —
When the fiery fight is heard no more,
  And the storm has ceased to blow.

XLIII

Old Ironsides

THE frigate *Constitution*, which had figured valiantly in the history of the United States navy, and had won the famous sea-fight with the English ship *Guerriere* in the War of 1812, was popularly called *Old Ironsides*, and had won a warm place in the hearts of the American people. On September 14, 1830, the *Boston Daily Advertiser* announced that the Secretary of the Navy had recommended that the *Constitution* be broken up, as no longer fit for service. As soon as he heard this Oliver Wendell Holmes wrote his poem *Old Ironsides*, which appeared two days later. It immediately became a battle-cry ; was repeated all through the country ; and caused such a wave of feeling for the time-scarred frigate that the plan of dismantling her was given up, and instead she was rebuilt, and given an honored place among the veterans of the country's navy.

OLD IRONSIDES

By Oliver Wendell Holmes

Ay, tear her tattered ensign down !
Long has it waved on high,
And many an eye has danced to see
That banner in the sky ;

Beneath it rung the battle shout,
　And burst the cannon's roar ;—
The meteor of the ocean air
　Shall sweep the clouds no more !

Her deck, once red with heroes' blood,
　Where knelt the vanquished foe,
When winds were hurrying o'er the flood
　And waves were white below,
No more shall feel the victor's tread,
　Or know the conquered knee ;—
The harpies of the shore shall pluck
　The eagle of the sea !

Oh, better that her shattered hulk
　Should sink beneath the wave ;
Her thunders shook the mighty deep,
　And there should be her grave ;
Nail to the mast her holy flag,
　Set every threadbare sail,
And give her to the God of storms,—
　The lightning and the gale !

THE CONSTITUTION AND THE GUERRIERE

XLIV

America

SAMUEL FRANCIS SMITH, a clergyman of Boston, was the author of "America," the song which is usually regarded as the national anthem of the United States. He himself said of it, "The song was written at Andover during my student life there, I think in the winter of 1831–32. It was first used publicly at a Sunday-school celebration on July 4th, in the Park Street Church, Boston. I had in my possession a quantity of German song-books, from which I was selecting such music as pleased me, and finding 'God Save the King,' I proceeded to give it the ring of American patriotism." Both the English anthem "God Save the King," and the American "My Country, 'tis of Thee," owe the air to which they are sung to Germany.

Oliver Wendell Holmes, who was a classmate at Harvard of the author of "America," referred to him aptly in one of the poems he wrote for a class reunion. Said Holmes:

> " And there's a nice youngster of excellent pith ;
> Fate tried to conceal him by naming him Smith !
> But he chanted a song for the brave and the free —
> Just read on his medal, ' My Country, of thee.' "

AMERICA

By Samuel Francis Smith

My country, 'tis of thee,
Sweet land of Liberty,
    Of thee I sing;
Land where my fathers died,
Land of the pilgrim's pride,
From every mountain side
    Let Freedom ring.

My native country, thee,
Land of the noble free,
    Thy name I love;
I love thy rocks and rills,
Thy woods and templed hills,
My heart with rapture thrills
    Like that above.

Let music swell the breeze,
And ring from all the trees
    Sweet Freedom's song;
Let mortal tongues awake;
Let all that breathe partake;
Let rocks their silence break,
    The sound prolong.

Our fathers' God, to Thee,
Author of Liberty,
    To Thee we sing;
Long may our land be bright
With Freedom's holy light;
Protect us by Thy might,
    Great God, our King.

Beneath Heaven's gracious will
The star of progress still
     Our course doth sway ;
In unity sublime
To broader heights we climb,
Triumphant over Time,
     God speeds our way !

Grand birthright of our sires,
Our altars and our fires
     Keep we still pure !
Our starry flag unfurled,
The hope of all the world,
In Peace and Light impearled,
     God hold secure !

XLV

Monterey

THE annexation of Texas by the United States in 1845 was regarded by Mexico as an act of war. That country immediately collected an army along the Rio Grande River, and General Zachary Taylor was sent into Texas with an army of occupation. Taylor found the Mexicans stationed at Matamoras. He threw up a line of entrenchments and built a fort opposite the Mexican batteries. While he was engaged elsewhere the Mexicans attacked this fort, and as soon as the news reached the American general he started back to relieve the small force at the fort. On his march he came upon the Mexican army, with six thousand men, drawn up before his army of twenty-one hundred soldiers, at Palo Alto. In spite of the difference in numbers Taylor attacked the enemy on May 8, 1846, and drove them back by the skilful firing of his artillery, and the repeated charges of his infantry.

The Mexican troops retreated to Resaca de la Palma. Taylor followed, attacked them again on the next day, routed them, and marched to the relief of the men in the fort.

The United States government now sent large reinforcements into Texas, and by the end of the summer General Taylor had a well-equipped army in the field.

Storming of Palace Hill at Battle of Monterey

The Mexican General Arista had brought ten thousand troops into the city of Monterey, which was supposed to be impregnable. Zachary Taylor marched on the city, and reached it September 19th. He found Monterey situated in a valley of the Sierra Madre Mountains, protected by the San Juan River and by a citadel whose guns commanded all the roads leading to the city.

The American army was deployed on all sides of the city, and began its attack on September 21st. For three days desperate fighting followed. The troops were cut to pieces by the cannon on the citadel, outlying heights were captured, only to be lost again when the Americans found they had no shelter from the Mexicans in the city. But finally the Americans gained a footing within the walls of Monterey. They had to fight across the barricades in the streets and through the houses and gardens. Gradually the Mexicans were dislodged and driven back and back, until on the evening of September 23d, Taylor's army succeeded in planting mortars in such a position that they could drop shells into any part of the city, and no shelter was left the defenders. Early in the morning of the 24th the Mexican general surrendered Monterey, having made terms of peace by which his army was allowed to evacuate the city with all the honors of war. The capture of Monterey cost the Americans five hundred men in killed and wounded, and the Mexicans fully twice as many.

The Mexican war finally ended in victory for the United States in February, 1848, after General Taylor had won the great victory of Buena Vista, and General Winfield Scott had carried the formidable fortress of Chapultepec and entered the City of Mexico, the capital of that country.

MONTEREY

By *Charles Fenno Hoffman*

We were not many—we who stood
　Before the iron sleet that day;
Yet many a gallant spirit would
Give half his years if but he could
　Have with us been at Monterey.

Now here, now there, the shot it hailed
　In deadly drifts of fiery spray,
Yet not a single soldier quailed
When wounded comrades round them wailed
　Their dying shout at Monterey.

And on—still on our column kept,
　Through walls of flame, its withering way;
Where fell the dead, the living stept,
Still charging on the guns which swept
　The slippery streets of Monterey.

The foe himself recoiled aghast,
　When, striking where he strongest lay,
We swooped his flanking batteries past,
And, braving full their murderous blast,
　Stormed home the towers of Monterey.

Our banners on those turrets wave,
    And there our evening bugles play ;
Where orange-boughs above their grave
Keep green the memory of the brave
    Who fought and fell at Monterey.

We are not many—we who pressed
    Beside the brave who fell that day;
But who of us has not confessed
He'd rather share their warrior rest
    Than not have been at Monterey ?

XLVI

The Charge of the Light Brigade

THIS famous charge occurred during the Crimean War, which was fought between the allied armies of England, France, Sardinia, and Turkey on the one side, and Russia on the other. The allied armies had invaded that part of southern Russia called the Crimea during the autumn of 1854, and were attempting to capture the very strongly fortified town and arsenal of Sevastopol. By the end of October, however, a very large Russian army was in the field, and the Russian general, Prince Menshikoff, determined to attack the allied forces. On October 25th, he opened fire on the rear of the British lines at Balaklava. This began a series of engagements, in which Sir Colin Campbell, with the 93d foot regiment, received and drove back a tremendous onslaught of Russian cavalry. At the same time General Scarlett, with the English Heavy Cavalry Brigade, completed Sir Colin's advantage by routing another part of the Russian army.

While this fighting was in progress a message was sent to Lord Cardigan, who commanded the English Light Brigade of Cavalry, to attack. Either through a misunderstanding of the message, or a blunder, he gave the word to try to take a Russian battery that was

The Charge of the Light Brigade

stationed at the far end of a long, narrow valley. This meant that the Light Brigade would have to run the gauntlet of two lines of infantry and artillery, as well as meet the full fire of the battery in their face.

The Light Brigade charged, although it was seen that the order was foolhardy in the extreme. Six hundred and seventy-three men went into action, but only one hundred and ninety-five returned unhurt.

The charge, although it made the battle of Balaklava famous, had little to do with the victory won by the English army. As the French said of it, " It was magnificent, but it was not warfare."

The report of the charge made a great sensation in England, and Tennyson, the Poet Laureate, wrote this poem of it. It is a fine war-chant, and the thunderous echo of the rhymes give it a charging effect like the actual galloping beats of the Light Brigade.

THE CHARGE OF THE LIGHT BRIGADE
By Alfred, Lord Tennyson

Half a league, half a league,
Half a league onward,
All in the valley of death
  Rode the six hundred.
Forward, the Light Brigade !
Charge for the guns, he said.
Into the valley of death
  Rode the six hundred.

Forward, the Light Brigade !
Was there a man dismay'd ?
Not though the soldiers knew
 Some one had blundered.
Theirs not to make reply,
Theirs not to reason why,
Theirs but to do and die.
Into the valley of death
 Rode the six hundred.

Cannon to right of them,
Cannon to left of them,
Cannon in front of them
 Volley'd and thunder'd ;
Storm'd at with shot and shell,
Boldly they rode and well.
Into the jaws of Death,
Into the mouth of Hell
 Rode the six hundred.

Flash'd all their sabres bare,
Flash'd as they turn'd in air,
Sabering the gunners there,
Charging an army, while
 All the world wonder'd :
Plunged in the battery-smoke,
Right through the line they broke ;
Cossack and Russian
Reel'd from the sabre-stroke
 Shatter'd and sunder'd.
Then they rode back, but not,
 Not the six hundred.

Cannon to right of them,
Cannon to left of them
Cannon behind them
  Volley'd and thunder'd ;
Storm'd at with shot and shell,
While horse and hero fell,
They that had fought so well
Came through the jaws of Death
Back from the mouth of Hell,
All that was left of them,
  Left of six hundred.

When can their glory fade ?
O, the wild charge they made !
  All the world wondered.
Honor the charge they made !
Honor the Light Brigade,
  Noble six hundred !

XLVII

The Relief of Lucknow

A GREAT revolt of the native soldiers in India against their English rulers occurred in 1857, and resulted in a wide-spread mutiny. The British East India Company, which then owned the greater part of India, had trained the Bengal natives to be soldiers, giving them Englishmen as officers. These native, or sepoy troops, as they were called, proved able fighting men, but in time the sepoys so largely outnumbered the English soldiers that they began to resist the orders of their officers. As soon as they found how powerful they were in numbers, they planned to overthrow the foreign rule.

The English had ordered the sepoys to use greased cartridges in their rifles, in spite of the fact that a native of Bengal would lose caste if he were to touch the fat of cows or pigs, and he would have to bite the greased cartridge to use it. Many of the soldiers in the barracks at Meerut, a military station near Delhi, refused to use these cartridges, and as a result were marched to prison. The next day, May 10, 1857, the native cavalry in Meerut armed, galloped to the prison, and released their comrades. Other regiments mutinied against their officers, and soon a large force of sepoys advanced to capture the important city of Delhi. The native soldiers there likewise turned on

THE RELIEF OF LUCKNOW

their English commanders, and Delhi became the centre of a great revolt.

In the meantime a mutiny had also broken out at Lucknow, in northern India, the capital of the province of Oudh. The sepoys deserted the English, and the British officers, together with all the English men, women, and children there, were forced to take refuge in the residency, or fort of Lucknow. Here a small number of fighting men held at bay a very large number of sepoy troops and a great rabble of natives. Food grew scarce, and fever, smallpox, and cholera spread among the little garrison. Week after week went by without succor, and the sepoys had almost undermined the fort, when, on September 25th, nearly three months after the siege had begun, a rescue party headed by General Havelock arrived and fought its way to the stockade. These reinforcements enabled the English to hold out until a much larger army under Sir Colin Campbell defeated the sepoys a month later and raised the siege.

For the period of almost three months before the arrival of Havelock the people in the fort at Lucknow had been the targets of a practically unceasing fire from heavy guns and muskets only fifty yards distant. The siege was one of the bravest and most remarkable in history.

The poem of its relief tells how a woman in the fort caught the first notes of the Scotch bagpipes playing "The Campbells are comin'," that told of Havelock's approach.

As a result of the Mutiny of 1857 the government of

India was transferred from the East India Company to the English crown.

THE RELIEF OF LUCKNOW
By Robert Trail Spence Lowell

Oh, that last day in Lucknow fort !
  We knew that it was the last ;
That the enemy's mines crept surely in,
  And the end was coming fast.

To yield to that foe meant worse than death ;
  And the men and we all worked on ;
It was one day more of smoke and roar,
  And then it would all be done.

There was one of us, a corporal's wife,
  A fair, young, gentle thing,
Wasted with fever in the siege,
  And her mind was wandering.

She lay on the ground, in her Scottish plaid,
  And I took her head on my knee ;
" When my father comes hame frae the pleugh,"
    she said,
  " Oh ! then please wauken me."

She slept like a child on her father's floor,
  In the flecking of woodbine shade,
When the house-dog sprawls by the open door,
  And the mother's wheel is stayed.

It was smoke and roar and powder-stench,
  And hopeless waiting for death;
And the soldier's wife, like a full-tired child,
  Seemed scarce to draw her breath.

I sank to sleep; and I had my dream
  Of an English village-lane,
And wall and garden; but one wild scream
  Brought me back to the roar again.

There Jessie Brown stood listening
  Till a sudden gladness broke
All over her face; and she caught my hand
  And drew me near and spoke:

"The Hielanders! Oh! dinna ye hear
  The slogan far awa?
The McGregor's? Oh! I ken it weel;
  It's the grandest o' them a'!

"God bless thae bonny Hielanders!
  We're saved! We're saved!" she cried;
And fell on her knees; and thanks to God
  Flowed forth like a full flood-tide.

Along the battery line her cry
  Had fallen among the men,
And they started back;—they were there to die;
  But was life so near them, then?

They listened for life; the rattling fire
  Far off, and the far-off roar,
Were all; and the colonel shook his head,
  And they turned to their guns once more.

Then Jessie said, "That slogan's done;
  But can ye hear them noo,
' *The Campbells are comin'* ' ?   It's no a dream;
  Our succors hae broken through."

We heard the roar and the rattle afar,
  But the pipes we could not hear;
So the men plied their work of hopeless war,
  And knew that the end was near.

It was not long ere it made its way,
  A thrilling, ceaseless sound:
It was no noise from the strife afar,
  Or the sappers under ground.

It *was* the pipes of the Highlanders!
  And now they played "*Auld Lang Syne.*"
It came to our men like the voice of God,
  And they shouted along the line.

And they wept, and shook one another's hands,
  And the women sobbed in a crowd;
And every one knelt down where he stood,
  And we all thanked God aloud.

That happy day, when we welcomed them,
  Our men put Jessie first;
And the general gave her his hand, and cheers
  Like a storm from the soldiers burst.

And the pipers' ribbons and tartan streamed,
  Marching round and round our line;
And our joyful cheers were broken with tears,
  As the pipes played "*Auld Lang Syne.*"

XLVIII

Battle-Hymn of the Republic

JULIA WARD HOWE was in Washington during the winter of 1861, when the question of the abolition of slavery was at fever-heat, and the outbreak of the Civil War at hand. She visited the soldiers encamped outside the city, and heard them singing "John Brown's Body." The majesty of the music to which those words were set struck her at once, and she determined to write new words that should be a hymn of patriotism. The opening line came to her easily, almost as if by inspiration, and she had completed the poem in a very short time. She took it back to Boston with her, and gave it to James T. Fields, editor of the *Atlantic Monthly*. He printed it on the first page of that magazine for February, 1862, giving it its present title.

The poem attracted very little attention at first, although it was copied into several newspapers. Then one of these newspapers was smuggled into Libby Prison in Richmond, Virginia; Chaplain Charles C. McCabe read the poem aloud to a few of the prisoners, and soon all the Union soldiers there were singing it.

As the Union prisoners were released they brought the hymn back to the North with them, and it spread in this fashion until it had become the most popular anthem on the Northern side.

For majesty of thought and beauty of word "The Battle-Hymn of the Republic" stands first among all the poems called forth by the Civil War, and among the first of all poems inspired by patriotism.

BATTLE-HYMN OF THE REPUBLIC
By Julia Ward Howe

Mine eyes have seen the glory of the coming of the Lord :
He is trampling out the vintage where the grapes of wrath are
    stored ;
He hath loosed the fateful lightning of His terrible swift sword :
        His truth is marching on.

I have seen Him in the watch-fires of a hundred circling camps ;
They have builded Him an altar in the evening's dews and
    damps ;
I have read His righteous sentence by the dim and flaring lamps.
        His day is marching on.

I have read a fiery gospel, writ in burnished rows of steel :
"As ye deal with my contemners, so with you my grace shall
    deal ;
Let the hero, born of woman, crush the serpent with his heel,
        Since God is marching on."

He has sounded forth the trumpet that shall never call retreat ;
He is sifting out the hearts of men before His judgment seat ;
Oh, be swift, my soul, to answer Him ! be jubilant, my feet !
        Our God is marching on.

In the beauty of the lilies, Christ was born across the sea,
With a glory in His bosom that transfigures you and me :
As He died to make men holy, let us die to make men free,
        While God is marching on.

Dixie's Land and Dixie

THE original song of "Dixie's Land" was written as a comic melody by Dan Emmett, a celebrated negro minstrel, in 1859. He is said to have taken the tune from an old plantation melody, and to have written verses to suit his audiences. When the Civil War began General Albert Pike wrote new words, calling on the South to arm and defend herself, and set these to the old air. The South at once claimed the song for her own, and it became the best loved of all the Southern ballads. Armies marched to it, and men went into battle singing it.

Many new verses have been written to the old melody, and the air is now as popular in the North as in the South. The words most generally associated with it now are those of the song by Dan Emmett, or variations on them, rather than the martial words of General Pike.

DIXIE'S LAND

I wish I was in de land ob cotton,
Cimmon seed an' sandy bottom —

In Dixie's Land whar I was born in,
Early on one frosty mornin'.

Look away—look away—Dixie Land.
Den I wish I was in Dixie, Hooray—Hooray !

In Dixie's Land we'll take our stand
To lib and die in Dixie.

Old Missus marry Will de weaber,
William was a gay deceaber.

When he put his arms around 'er,
He look as fierce as a forty pounder.

His face was sharp like butcher's cleaber,
But dat didn't seem to grieb her ;

Will run away—Missus took a decline, oh,
Her face was de color ob bacon rine—oh.

How could she act such a foolish part
As marry a man dat break her heart ?

Here's a health to de next old Missus,
And all de gals dat wants to kiss us.

Now if you want to dribe away sorrow,
Come and hear dis song to-morrow !

Sugar in de gourd and stonny batter,
De whites grow fat an' de niggers fatter !

Den hoe it down and scratch your grabble,
To Dixie's Land I am bound to trabble.

Look away—look away—Dixie Land.
Den I wish I was in Dixie.   Hooray ! Hooray !

DIXIE

By Albert Pike

Southrons, hear your country call you !
Up, lest worse than death befall you !
   To arms !   To arms !   To arms, in Dixie !
Lo ! all the beacon-fires are lighted,—
Let all hearts be now united !
   To arms !   To arms !   To arms, in Dixie !
      Advance the flag of Dixie !
         Hurrah ! hurrah !
For Dixie's land we take our stand,
      And live and die for Dixie !
         To arms !   To arms !
      And conquer peace for Dixie !
         To arms !   To arms !
      And conquer peace for Dixie !

Hear the Northern thunders mutter !
Northern flags in South winds flutter !
Send them back your fierce defiance !
Stamp upon the accursed alliance !

Fear no danger !   Shun no labor !
Lift up rifle, pike, and sabre !
Shoulder pressing close to shoulder,
Let the odds make each heart bolder !

How the South's great heart rejoices
At your cannon's ringing voices !
For faith betrayed, and pledges broken,
Wrongs inflicted, insults spoken.

Strong as lions, swift as eagles,
Back to their kennels hunt these beagles!
Cut the unequal bonds asunder!
Let them hence each other plunder!

Swear upon your country's altar
Never to submit or falter,
Till the spoilers are defeated,
Till the Lord's work is completed!

Halt not till our Federation
Secures among earth's powers its station!
Then at peace, and crowned with glory,
Hear your children tell the story!

If the loved ones weep in sadness,
Victory soon shall bring them gladness,—
  To arms!
Exultant pride soon vanish sorrow;
Smiles chase tears away to-morrow.
  To arms!   To arms!   To arms, in Dixie!
   Advance the flag of Dixie!
    Hurrah!   Hurrah!
For Dixie's land we take our stand,
   And live or die for Dixie!
    To arms!   To arms!
   And conquer peace for Dixie!
    To arms!   To arms!
   And conquer peace for Dixie!

LI

My Maryland

THIS song shared popularity with "Dixie" among the Southern soldiers during the Civil War. At the outbreak of the war it was not certain whether the state of Maryland would remain in the Union or would secede. Feeling ran high in Baltimore, and when the Sixth Massachusetts regiment arrived in that city on April 19, 1861, on its way to Washington, crowds of Confederate sympathizers filled the streets and attacked the troops. The soldiers finally had to fire to secure their safety, and a number of citizens were killed and more wounded.

This roused even greater resentment among those who wanted Maryland to secede. The Federal government at once sent troops under General Butler to Baltimore and Annapolis, and the Union party, which was actually much stronger than the Confederate party in the state, held Maryland to the Union.

The author of "My Maryland" wrote the poem immediately on hearing of the attack at Baltimore, and when it was thought that Maryland might secede. He was of course an ardent Confederate sympathizer. Miss Hattie Cary of Baltimore set the words to the old college air of "Lauriger Horatius," and it soon became almost as popular around Southern camp-fires as " Dixie."

MY MARYLAND

By James Ryder Randall

The despot's heel is on thy shore,
    Maryland !
His torch is at thy temple door,
    Maryland !
Avenge the patriotic gore
That flecked the streets of Baltimore
And be the battle queen of yore,
    Maryland, my Maryland !

Hark to an exiled son's appeal,
    Maryland !
My mother State, to thee I kneel,
    Maryland !
For life or death, for woe or weal,
Thy peerless chivalry reveal,
And gird thy beauteous limbs with steel,
    Maryland, my Maryland !

Thou wilt not cower in the dust,
    Maryland !
Thy beaming sword shall never rust,
    Maryland !
Remember Carroll's sacred trust,
Remember Howard's warlike thrust,
And all thy slumberers with the just,
    Maryland, my Maryland !

Come! 'tis the red dawn of the day,
     Maryland!
Come with thy panoplied array,
     Maryland!
With Ringgold's spirit for the fray,
With Watson's blood at Monterey,
With fearless Lowe and dashing May,
     Maryland, my Maryland!

Dear Mother, burst the tyrant's chain,
     Maryland!
Virginia shall not call in vain,
     Maryland!
She meets her sisters on the plain,
"*Sic semper!*" 'tis the proud refrain
That baffles minions back amain,
     Maryland!
Arise in majesty again,
     Maryland, my Maryland!

Come! for thy shield is bright and strong,
     Maryland!
Come! for thy dalliance does thee wrong,
     Maryland!
Come to thy own heroic throng
Stalking with Liberty along,
And chant thy dauntless slogan-song,
     Maryland, my Maryland!

I see the blush upon thy cheek,
     Maryland!
But thou wast ever bravely meek,
     Maryland!

But lo ! there surges forth a shriek,
From hill to hill, from creek to creek,
Potomac calls to Chesapeake,
        Maryland, my Maryland !

Thou wilt not yield to Vandal toll,
        Maryland !
Thou wilt not crook to his control,
        Maryland !
Better the fire upon thee roll,
Better the shot, the blade, the bowl,
Than crucifixion of the soul,
        Maryland, my Maryland !

I hear the distant thunder-hum,
        Maryland !
The " Old Line's " bugle, fife, and drum ;
        Maryland !
She is not dead, nor deaf, nor dumb ;
Huzza ! she spurns the Northern scum —
She breathes ! She burns ! She'll come ! She'll
        come !
        Maryland, my Maryland !

LII

The *Cumberland*

EARLY in 1862 a war-ship made her appearance at Hampton Roads, off Fortress Monroe, in Virginia, which was destined to change the naval battles of the future. The vessel was a Confederate ironclad called the *Merrimac*. An old ship had been altered by having a wedge-shaped prow of cast-iron project about two feet in front of the bow, and covering a wooden roof which sloped to the water-line with two iron plates of armor. A battery of ten guns was placed inside the ironclad. So constructed, it was thought that the new type of war-ship could readily destroy the old-fashioned Union frigates, and herself escape without injury.

Five Union ships, the fifty gun frigate *Congress*, the twenty-four gun sloop *Cumberland*, and the frigates *St. Lawrence*, *Roanoke*, and *Minnesota*, lay near Newport News on March 8, 1862, when about noon the new ship *Merrimac* suddenly appeared from the James River. The three nearest frigates, believing they could easily defeat the stranger, immediately slipped their cables, but, as all were of deep draft, shortly grounded in shallow water. The two other Union ships, together with the shore batteries, opened fire upon the strange black vessel that looked like a crocodile or some unknown sea-monster. To their surprise the shot bounced off the sloping back of the ironclad like rubber balls, and seemed to do no damage.

Lieutenant George Upham Morris was in command of the *Cumberland*, and as he saw the strange ship advancing to attack him he ordered broadsides of shot and shell poured at her. The heavy fire had no effect. The monster steamed on, and rammed her iron prow into the wooden side of the *Cumberland*. The frigate sank in fifty-five minutes, carrying down officers and crew, one hundred and twenty-five in all. Her flag was still flying as she sank, and her guns fired even when the water had reached the gunwales.

The *Merrimac* then turned to the *Congress*, which had made for the shore, and riddled her with shot until she caught on fire, and an exploding powder-magazine destroyed her. The *Merrimac* finally retired at nightfall to the shelter of the Confederate batteries, having spread consternation through the Union fleet.

Next morning, however, when the victorious *Merrimac* steamed out to destroy the three remaining frigates, she found that a tiny vessel named the *Monitor* had arrived at Hampton Roads over night, and was ready to meet her. This *Monitor* showed only a thin edge of surface above the water-line, and an iron turret revolved in sight, from which two guns could be fired in any direction. As the Northern papers said, this ship looked like a "cheese-box on a raft."

The Goliath of a *Merrimac* advanced to meet the David of a *Monitor*, and a three hours' battle followed. Neither could force the other to surrender, but finally the larger ironclad began to leak and had to with-

The Merrimac and the Monitor

draw, leaving the little *Monitor* in possession of the Roads.

This marked the beginning of the change from wooden ships-of-war to ironclads.

THE *CUMBERLAND*
By Henry Wadsworth Longfellow

At anchor in Hampton Roads we lay,
  On board of the *Cumberland*, sloop-of-war ;
And at times from the fortress across the bay
    The alarum of drums swept past,
    Or a bugle blast
  From the camp on the shore.

Then far away to the south uprose
  A little feather of snow-white smoke,
And we knew that the iron ship of our foes
    Was steadily steering its course
    To try the force
  Of our ribs of oak.

Down upon us heavily runs,
  Silent and sullen, the floating fort ;
Then comes a puff of smoke from her guns,
    And leaps the terrible death,
    With fiery breath,
  From each open port.

We are not idle, but send her straight
  Defiance back in a full broadside !
As hail rebounds from a roof of slate,
    Rebounds our heavier hail
    From each iron scale
  Of the monster's hide.

"Strike your flag!" the rebel cries,
  In his arrogant old plantation strain.
"Never!" our gallant Morris replies;
    "It is better to sink than to yield!"
    And the whole air pealed
  With the cheers of our men.

Then, like a kraken huge and black,
  She crushed our ribs in her iron grasp!
Down went the *Cumberland* all a wrack,
    With a sudden shudder of death,
    And the cannon's breath
  For her dying gasp.

Next morn, as the sun rose over the bay,
  Still floated our flag at the mainmast head.
Lord, how beautiful was Thy day!
    Every waft of the air
    Was a whisper of prayer,
  Or a dirge for the dead.

Ho! brave hearts that went down in the seas!
  Ye are at peace in the troubled stream;
Ho! brave land! with hearts like these,
    Thy flag, that is rent in twain,
    Shall be one again,
  And without a seam!

LIII

Stonewall Jackson's Way

" STONEWALL " was a nickname given to Thomas J. Jackson, a lieutenant-general in the Confederate army, who was one of the ablest and bravest commanders who took part in the Civil War. Early in the war he was ordered to reinforce the army of General Beauregard, who was fighting at Manassas. He did so, and in the battle that followed the Union army came very near routing the Southern troops by a desperate charge. Jackson and his brigade stood firm, and General Lee, seeing him, called out to his own wavering men, "Look at Jackson—there he stands like a stone wall ; rally behind the Virginians ! " The other brigades obeyed the order, and eventually the Confederates carried the day. It was in this way that Jackson and his men won the nickname of " Stonewall Jackson " and the "Stonewall Brigade " that came to be a badge of honor in later campaigns.

"Stonewall Jackson " was a strict Presbyterian and a man of unusual religious feeling. He had graduated at West Point, fought in the Mexican War, and then taught in the Virginia Military Institute at Lexington. There he had been called " The Blue-Light Elder " by his pupils, who were very fond of him, and the name was sometimes used by his soldiers after the Civil War began.

The general was a dashing leader, and his men would follow him anywhere. He rose rapidly in rank, and in a short time had become General Lee's chief mainstay. Many a Confederate victory was due to his personal courage in leading his troops at a decisive moment in battle, and time and again his "Stonewall Brigade" turned a seeming rout into victory.

In the spring of 1863 the Union and Confederate armies prepared to renew the struggle that the winter had partly interrupted. The Union General Hooker crossed the Rappahannock River on April 28th, for the purpose of attacking the Confederates who were near Fredericksburg. The entire Union Army of the Potomac had crossed the river and bivouacked at Chancellorsville by the night of April 30th. The Confederate General Lee at once prepared to attack Hooker, and early on May 1st he sent "Stonewall Jackson," in command of thirty-three thousand men, towards Chancellorsville.

The two armies made ready on that day, some fighting occurring, but the real battle of Chancellorsville did not begin until May 2d. Late on that afternoon Jackson, who had made a flank movement, burst from the woods and routed the Union right wing. At this point General Pleasanton hurled the Eighth Pennsylvania Cavalry under Major Keenan, on the Confederate flank. Keenan charged again and again, losing most of his men, but giving the Union artillery time to get into position and fire.

The Confederates were checked by this firing, and Jackson and his staff rode forward to look at the field. As he was riding back to his own lines the general and his companions were mistaken for Union horsemen by his own soldiers and were fired at. Jackson was shot, and died on May 10th. The Confederates won the fighting at Chancellorsville after several days of battle, but the victory was largely offset by the loss of one of their very greatest generals.

The poem, "Stonewall Jackson's Way," is said to have been written within hearing of the battle of Antietam, September 17, 1862, and was found in the coat of a dead soldier of the "Stonewall Brigade," after one of Jackson's battles in the Shenandoah Valley. It became very popular, but its authorship was unknown until almost twenty-five years later.

STONEWALL JACKSON'S WAY
By John Williamson Palmer

Come, stack arms, men ! Pile on the rails,
    Stir up the camp-fire bright ;
No matter if the canteen fails,
    We'll make a roaring night.
Here Shenandoah brawls along,
There burly Blue Ridge echoes strong,
To swell the brigade's rousing song
    Of "Stonewall Jackson's way."

We see him now,—the old slouched hat
    Cocked o'er his eye askew ;
The shrewd, dry smile, the speech so pat,
    So calm, so blunt, so true.

The " Blue-Light Elder " knows 'em well ;
Says he, " That's Banks,—he's fond of shell ;
Lord save his soul ! we'll give him ——; " well,
   That's "Stonewall Jackson's way."

Silence ! ground arms ! kneel all ! caps off !
   Old " Blue Light's " going to pray.
Strangle the fool that dares to scoff !
   Attention ! it's his way.
Appealing from his native sod,
In forma pauperis to God,
" Lay bare Thine arm ; stretch forth Thy rod !
   Amen ! "   That's "Stonewall's way."

He's in the saddle now.   Fall in !
   Steady ! the whole brigade !
Hill's at the ford cut off ; we'll win
   His way out, ball and blade !
What matter if our shoes are worn ?
What matter if our feet are torn ?
" Quick-step ! we're with him before morn ! "
   That's " Stonewall Jackson's way."

The sun's bright lances rout the mists
   Of morning, and, by George !
Here's Longstreet struggling in the lists,
   Hemmed in an ugly gorge.
Pope and his Yankees, whipped before,
" Bay'nets and grape ! " hear Stonewall roar ;
" Charge, Stuart !   Pay off Ashby's score ! "
   In " Stonewall Jackson's way."

Ah ! Maiden, wait and watch and yearn
   For news of Stonewall's band !
Ah ! Widow, read, with eyes that burn,
   That ring upon thy hand.

Ah ! Wife, sew on, pray on, hope on ;
Thy life shall not be all forlorn ;
The foe had better ne'er been born
    That gets in " Stonewall's way."

LIV

Barbara Frietchie

EARLY in the Civil War, in September, 1862, General Robert E. Lee of the Confederate army succeeded in crossing the Potomac River, and planned to march on Baltimore or Philadelphia. On this march he entered Frederick City, Maryland, September 13th.

According to Whittier's poem there were forty American flags flying in the town, but the Confederate sympathizers pulled them down as Lee's army entered. Then an old woman named Barbara Frietchie took one of the flags and fastened it to a staff outside her attic window. General " Stonewall " Jackson saw the flag as he marched past with his men, and gave the order to fire. But even as the flag fell from the staff Barbara Frietchie seized it. She cried to them all, "Shoot, if you must, this old gray head, but spare your country's flag ! "

Jackson recognized her courage, and was stirred by it. He gave his men the order to march, and all day the flag flew from that attic window as Lee's army went through the streets of Frederick City.

The story of Barbara Frietchie has been accepted as true by several historians, but there is some doubt as to whether the facts were exactly similar to the account in the poem. Whittier himself said that he had the story from trustworthy sources. In a note to the poem he wrote : " It is admitted by all that Barbara Frietchie was no myth, but a worthy and highly esteemed gentle-woman, intensely loyal and a hater of the Slavery Rebellion, holding her Union flag sacred and keeping it with her Bible ; that when the Confederates halted before her house, and entered her dooryard, she denounced them in vigorous language, shook her cane in their faces, and drove them out ; and when General Burnside's troops followed close upon Jackson's, she waved her flag and cheered them. It is stated that May Quantrell, a brave and loyal lady in another part of the city, did wave her flag in sight of the Confederates. It is possible that there has been a blending of the two incidents."

BARBARA FRIETCHIE
By John Greenleaf Whittier

Up from the meadows rich with corn,
Clear in the cool September morn,

The clustered spires of Frederick stand
Green-walled by the hills of Maryland.

Round about them orchards sweep,
Apple and peach tree fruited deep,

Fair as a garden of the Lord
To the eyes of the famished rebel horde,

On that pleasant morn of the early fall
When Lee marched over the mountain wall,—

Over the mountains, winding down,
Horse and foot into Frederick town.

Forty flags with their silver stars,
Forty flags with their crimson bars,

Flapped in the morning wind : the sun
Of noon looked down, and saw not one.

Up rose old Barbara Frietchie then,
Bowed with her fourscore years and ten ;

Bravest of all in Frederick town,
She took up the flag the men hauled down ;

In her attic window the staff she set,
To show that one heart was loyal yet.

Up the street came the rebel tread,
Stonewall Jackson riding ahead.

Under his slouched hat left and right
He glanced ; the old flag met his sight.

" Halt ! "—the dust-brown ranks stood fast.
" Fire ! "—out blazed the rifle-blast.

It shivered the window, pane and sash ;
It rent the banner with seam and gash.

Quick, as it fell, from the broken staff
Dame Barbara snatched the silken scarf ;

She leaned far out on the window sill,
And shook it forth with a royal will.

" Shoot, if you must, this old gray head,
But spare your country's flag," she said.

A shade of sadness, a blush of shame,
Over the face of the leader came;

The nobler nature within him stirred
To life at that woman's deed and word:

" Who touches a hair of yon gray head
Dies like a dog !   March on ! " he said.

All day long through Frederick street
Sounded the tread of marching feet :

All day long that free flag tost
Over the heads of the rebel host.

Ever its torn folds rose and fell
On the loyal winds that loved it well ;

And through the hill-gaps sunset light
Shone over it with a warm good-night.

Barbara Frietchie's work is o'er,
And the rebel rides on his raids no more.

Honor to her ! and let a tear
Fall, for her sake, on " Stonewall's " bier.

Over Barbara Frietchie's grave,
Flag of freedom and union, wave !

Peace, and order, and beauty draw
Round thy symbol of light and law ;

And ever the stars above look down
On thy stars below in Frederick town !

LV

High Tide at Gettysburg

THE battle of Gettysburg, fought during the three days of July first, second, and third, 1863, marked the turning-point in the American Civil War. The Confederate armies were making headway northward, and the Union troops, veteran though they were, had been outmanœuvered time and again during the spring of that year. In spite of General Hooker's efforts, the Confederates under General Robert E. Lee crossed into Pennsylvania, and it looked as if that state would shortly be at the mercy of the invading army. There was panic at the North. President Lincoln called out 100,000 militia, and the Union General Hooker started to try to catch and check Lee. On June 27th, however, Hooker was relieved of the command at his own request, and General George G. Meade was appointed in command of the army.

The two great armies, largely ignorant of each other's plans, drew near each other during the end of June. Longstreet and Hill, of the Confederate army, had turned eastward, and Meade, having brought the Army of the Potomac across Maryland, was headed towards the enemy at right angles. Lee decided to collect his forces at the Pennsylvania town of Gettysburg, and there his advance guard happened to come into contact with the Union troops on the morning of July first.

Gettysburg lies in a hilly country, a valley dotted with farms, protected by two ridges, Seminary Ridge on the west, and Cemetery Ridge on the southeast. This latter range begins in a cliff called Culp's Hill, and at its southern end towers a high rock known as Round Top. General Reynolds of the Union army was the first corps commander to reach Gettysburg, and as soon as he discovered that the bulk of the Confederate army was at hand he decided to join battle with them and so gain time for General Meade to mass his main army and prepare to check the enemy. In the first day's encounter the Confederates won the advantage, General Reynolds was killed, and the Union lines were swept back to the line of Cemetery Ridge.

General Lee reached Gettysburg that evening, and General Meade hurriedly brought up the scattered corps of his great army. Lee decided to attack where they were, although he had not chosen the field, and in the afternoon of July second the battle was renewed and in spite of the intense heat both armies fought with undiminished fury. The Confederates won several slight advantages, but on the whole the second day's battle was inconclusive, and the Union forces still held their lines in unbroken order.

Lee determined to renew his attack on the third day, and Meade planned to stay and receive it. Both armies spent the morning in preparation. In the afternoon Lee ordered the advance, and the Confederates charged across the valley in a line three miles long. General George Pickett, with his Virginians, supported by the men of Pettigrew, Wilcox, and

Trimble, led the van, and bore the brunt of the great charge. Five thousand men under Pickett dashed against the entrenched Union lines, and though they had to face a withering fire, charged up to the very front of their enemy, and grappled with them. For a moment they gained a foothold, then the Union soldiers, massing at this crucial point, flung them back, and the charge was ended. More than two thousand men had been killed or wounded in thirty minutes. Pickett gave the order to retreat, and as his men fell back the Union soldiers sprang forward, and pursued a short distance, taking many prisoners and battle ensigns.

The Union army had also repulsed the Confederates in other parts of the field, and the day ended in victory for Meade's men. During the night Lee retreated in good order.

The Confederates never penetrated as far north again, and the point that Pickett reached at the height of his charge is often called the " High Water Mark of the Confederacy." The charge, though ill-advised, was heroically carried out, and has become famous as one of the bravest events in the Civil War.

HIGH TIDE AT GETTYSBURG

By Will Henry Thompson

A cloud possessed the hollow field,
The gathering battle's smoky shield :
  Athwart the gloom the lightning flashed,
    And through the cloud some horsemen dashed,
And from the heights the thunder pealed.

Then, at the brief command of Lee
Moved out that matchless infantry,
   With Pickett leading grandly down,
   To rush against the roaring crown
Of those dread heights of destiny.

Far heard above the angry guns,
A cry across the tumult runs ;
   The voice that rang through Shiloh's woods
   And Chickamauga's solitudes,
The fierce South cheering on her sons !

Ah, how the withering tempest blew
Against the front of Pettigrew !
   A Khamsin wind that scorched and singed
   Like that infernal flame that fringed
The British squares at Waterloo !

A thousand fell where Kemper led ;
A thousand died where Garnett bled :
   In blinding flame and strangling smoke
   The remnant through the batteries broke
And crossed the works with Armistead.

"Once more in Glory's van with me !"
Virginia cried to Tennessee :
   "We two together, come what may,
   Shall stand upon these works to-day ! "
The reddest day in history.

Brave Tennessee !   In reckless way
Virginia heard her comrades say :
   "Close round this rent and riddled rag ! "
   What time she set her battle-flag
Amid the guns of Doubleday.

But who shall break the guards that wait
Before the awful face of Fate?
　　The tattered standards of the South
　　Were shrivelled at the cannon's mouth,
And all her hopes were desolate.

In vain the Tennesseean set
His breast against the bayonet;
　　In vain Virginia charged and raged,
　　A tigress in her wrath uncaged,
Till all the hill was red and wet!

Above the bayonets, mixed and crossed,
Men saw a gray, gigantic ghost
　　Receding through the battle-cloud,
　　And heard across the tempest loud
The death-cry of a nation lost!

The brave went down! Without disgrace
They leaped to Ruin's red embrace;
　　They only heard Fame's thunders wake,
　　And saw the dazzling sunburst break
In smiles on Glory's bloody face!

They fell, who lifted up a hand
And bade the sun in heaven to stand;
　　They smote and fell, who set the bars
　　Against the progress of the stars,
And stayed the march of Motherland.

They stood, who saw the future come
On through the fight's delirium;
　　They smote and stood, who held the hope
　　Of nations on that slippery slope,
Amid the cheers of Christendom!

God lives !   He forged the iron will,
That clutched and held that trembling hill !
  God lives and reigns !   He built and lent
  The heights for Freedom's battlement,
Where floats her flag in triumph still !

Fold up the banner !   Smelt the guns !
Love rules.   Her gentler purpose runs.
  A mighty mother turns in tears,
  The pages of her battle years,
Lamenting all her fallen sons !

LVI

John Burns of Gettysburg

MORE than 160,000 men fought in the three days' battle of Gettysburg, and among them was John Burns, an old veteran of the War of 1812 and the Mexican War, who had volunteered for service at the outbreak of the Civil War, but had been rejected on account of his age. He was seventy years old in 1863.

John Burns had volunteered among the first in the War of 1812, and had fought at the battles of Platts-burg, Queenstown, and Lundy's Lane. He served through the Mexican campaign, and when he volun-teered in 1861, had been told that he was too old, but was given work as a teamster. Finally he was sent back to his home at Gettysburg, where his neighbors made him the town constable. But his heart was set on fighting for the Union, and when the Confederates came to Gettysburg late in June, 1863, he made so much trouble for them that he was put under restraint. When the Confederates left the town he tried to arrest stragglers from their army by virtue of his office of constable.

When the actual fighting began on July 1st John Burns could not keep away from the battle. He borrowed a rifle and ammunition from a wounded Union soldier, and, marching to headquarters, volunteered for service.   The Colonel of the Seventh Wisconsin Regiment gave him a long-range rifle, and he took up a position on a height from which he did sharpshooting with deadly effect during that day.

When the Union forces were driven back at sunset Burns was badly wounded and was finally captured by the enemy.   He had a narrow escape from being hanged as a combatant in civilian's clothes.   After the battle he was released, and returned to his home, where thousands of visitors came to see him later to hear his account of the great struggle.

Bret Harte took the incidents of John Burns' part in the battle, and made a stirring poem of the old man's unquenchable patriotism.

JOHN BURNS OF GETTYSBURG
By Bret Harte

Have you heard the story that gossips tell
Of Burns of Gettysburg?—No?   Ah, well :
Brief is the glory that hero earns,
Briefer the story of poor John Burns :
He was the fellow who won renown,—
The only man who didn't back down
When the rebels rode through his native town ;
But held his own in the fight next day,
When all his townsfolk ran away.
That was in July, Sixty-three,
The very day that General Lee,
Flower of Southern chivalry,
Baffled and beaten, backward reeled
From a stubborn Meade and a barren field.

I might tell how but the day before
John Burns stood at his cottage door,
Looking down the village street,
Where, in the shade of his peaceful vine,
He heard the low of his gathered kine,
And felt their breath with incense sweet;
Or I might say, when the sunset burned
The old farm gable, he thought it turned
The milk that fell like a babbling flood
Into the milk-pail red as blood!
Or how he fancied the hum of bees
Were bullets buzzing among the trees.
But all such fanciful thoughts as these
Were strange to a practical man like Burns,
Who minded only his own concerns,
Troubled no more by fancies fine
Than one of his calm-eyed, long-tailed, kine,—
Quite old-fashioned and matter-of-fact,
Slow to argue, but quick to act.
That was the reason, as some folks say,
He fought so well on that terrible day.

And it was terrible.   On the right
Raged for hours the heady fight,
Thundered the battery's double bass,—
Difficult music for men to face;
While on the left—where now the graves
Undulate like the living waves
That all that day unceasing swept
Up to the pits the Rebels kept—
Round shot ploughed the upland glades,
Sown with bullets, reaped with blades;
Shattered fences here and there
Tossed their splinters in the air;
The very trees were stripped and bare;

The barns that once held yellow grain
Were heaped with harvests of the slain ;
The cattle bellowed on the plain,
The turkeys screamed with might and main,
And brooding barn-fowl left their rest
With strange shells bursting in each nest.

Just where the tide of battle turns,
Erect and lonely stood old John Burns.
How do you think the man was dressed ?
He wore an ancient long buff vest,
Yellow as saffron,—but his best ;
And, buttoned over his manly breast,
Was a bright blue coat, with a rolling collar,
And large gilt buttons,—size of a dollar,—
With tails that the country-folk called "swaller."
He wore a broad-brimmed, bell-crowned hat,
White as the locks on which it sat.
Never had such a sight been seen
For forty years on the village green,
Since old John Burns was a country beau,
And went to the " quiltings " long ago.

Close at his elbows all that day,
Veterans of the Peninsula,
Sunburnt and bearded, charged away ;
And striplings, downy of lip and chin,—
Clerks that the Home Guard mustered in,—
Glanced, as they passed, at the hat he wore,
Then at the rifle his right hand bore ;
And hailed him, from out their youthful lore,
With scraps of a slangy *répertoire :*
"How are you, White Hat?" "Put her through!"
"Your head's level!" and "Bully for you!"

Called him "Daddy,"—begged he'd disclose
The name of the tailor who made his clothes,
And what was the value he set on those;
While Burns, unmindful of jeer and scoff,
Stood there picking the rebels off,—
With his long brown rifle and bell-crown hat,
And the swallow-tails they were laughing at.

'Twas but a moment, for that respect
Which clothes all courage their voices checked;
And something the wildest could understand
Spake in the old man's strong right hand,
And his corded throat, and the lurking frown
Of his eyebrows under his old bell-crown;
Until, as they gazed, there crept an awe
Through the ranks in whispers, and some men saw,
In the antique vestments and long white hair,
The Past of the Nation in battle there;
And some of the soldiers since declare
That the gleam of his old white hat afar,
Like the crested plume of the brave Navarre,
That day was their oriflamme of war.

So raged the battle.   You know the rest:
How the rebels, beaten and backward pressed,
Broke at the final charge, and ran.
At which John Burns—a practical man—
Shouldered his rifle, unbent his brows,
And then went back to his bees and cows.

That is the story of old John Burns;
This is the moral the reader learns:
In fighting the battle, the question's whether
You'll show a hat that's white, or a feather!

LVII

Sheridan's Ride

AT the end of the summer of 1864 the Confederate cavalry were pushing north into Pennsylvania, making for the Susquehanna River. They sacked the town of Chambersburg, and threw the neighboring country into panic. General Grant at once sent a large force to head off this invasion, and placed General Philip Henry Sheridan in command of it. On September 19, 1864, the Confederate General Early attacked Sheridan's troops at Winchester. Sheridan defeated Early after repeated charges by the Union cavalry, and sent him retreating down the Shenandoah Valley.

This repulse was thought to have checked General Early, and a little later Sheridan went to Washington to consult with the Secretary of War. During his absence, on October 18th, the Confederates secretly moved a large force against the Union army at Cedar Creek, and the following morning attacked the sleeping camp in front, flank, and rear. The Federal troops, taken absolutely by surprise, broke and fled. Early drove them before him, and appeared to be winning a great victory. But Sheridan was returning from Washington, and had reached the town of Winchester when he heard the sound of cannon. He instantly put spurs to his horse and dashed towards Cedar Creek, a distance of twenty miles.

As the general came up to his retreating men he shouted, "Face the other way, boys; we're going back!" The soldiers turned and followed him, and by the time he reached the battle-field at noon the retreating army was turned into an attacking one. Cheering for Sheridan the soldiers charged and completely routed Early's army, driving them back again and out of the Valley. Sheridan's ride won a great Union victory, and in recognition of it President Lincoln made the commander a major-general.

SHERIDAN'S RIDE

By Thomas Buchanan Read

Up from the South at break of day,
Bringing to Winchester fresh dismay,
The affrighted air with a shudder bore,
Like a herald in haste, to the chieftain's door,
The terrible grumble, and rumble, and roar,
Telling the battle was on once more,
And Sheridan twenty miles away.

And wider still those billows of war
Thundered along the horizon's bar;
And louder yet into Winchester rolled
The roar of that red sea uncontrolled,
Making the blood of the listener cold,
As he thought of the stake in that fiery fray,
And Sheridan twenty miles away.

But there is a road from Winchester town,
A good, broad highway leading down;
And there, through the flush of the morning light,
A steed as black as the steeds of night,
Was seen to pass, as with eagle flight.
As if he knew the terrible need,
He stretched away with his utmost speed;
Hills rose and fell; but his heart was gay,
With Sheridan fifteen miles away.

Still sprung from those swift hoofs, thundering south,
The dust, like smoke from the cannon's mouth;
Or the trail of a comet, sweeping faster and faster,
Foreboding to traitors the doom of disaster.
The heart of the steed, and the heart of the master
Were beating like prisoners assaulting their walls,
Impatient to be where the battle-field calls;
Every nerve of the charger was strained to full play
With Sheridan only ten miles away.

Under his spurning feet, the road
Like an arrowy Alpine river flowed,
And the landscape sped away behind
Like an ocean flying before the wind,
And the steed, like a bark fed with furnace ire,
Swept on, with his wild eye full of fire.
But, lo! he is nearing his heart's desire;
He is snuffing the smoke of the roaring fray,
With Sheridan only five miles away.

The first that the general saw were the groups
Of stragglers, and then the retreating troops;
What was done? what to do? a glance told him both,
Then striking his spurs with a terrible oath,

He dashed down the line, 'mid a storm of huzzas,
And the wave of retreat checked its course there, becau
The sight of the master compelled it to pause.
With foam and with dust the black charger was gray;
By the flash of his eye, and his red nostril's play,
He seemed to the whole great army to say,
" I have brought you Sheridan all the way,
From Winchester down, to save the day."

Hurrah, hurrah for Sheridan !
Hurrah, hurrah for horse and man !
And when their statues are placed on high,
Under the dome of the Union sky,—
The American soldiers' Temple of Fame,
There, with the glorious general's name,
Be it said, in letters both bold and bright :
" Here is the steed that saved the day
By carrying Sheridan into the fight,
From Winchester,—twenty miles away ! "

LVIII

Marching Through Georgia

By the middle of the fourth year of the Civil War, in 1864, the Union forces had grown far superior to the Confederates in numbers and resources. The Northern armies numbered eight hundred thousand men, while the Southern had barely half that many. The Confederates were therefore largely compelled to keep on the defensive.

It was thought that the Federal army could now crush the Confederates by one great effort. General Ulysses S. Grant had shown himself the most successful commander on the Northern side, and he was made lieutenant-general and given entire direction of the campaign. He decided to march towards Richmond, and ordered General William Tecumseh Sherman to take Atlanta.

Sherman had an army of veterans, and advanced rapidly south. By the middle of July, 1864, he was in front of Atlanta. The Confederates tried to break through his lines, but were thrown back. On July 22d Sherman ordered an attack on the city, and the fighting lasted for two days, with both armies losing many men. The Union troops could not take Atlanta by assault, and so settled down to tire out the Confederates. For almost a month daily skirmishes followed, and on September 2d, the Southern armies evacuated the city.

When he had possession of Atlanta Sherman decided on a manœuvre which was to have a great effect on the war. He planned to destroy Atlanta, and march through the state of Georgia, capturing one or more of the large seaport cities. He burned Atlanta, and set his army on march for Savannah on November 16, 1864.

This was the famous "march to the sea," which divided the Confederate country and despoiled the homes and farms of Georgia. The army left a track of ruin forty miles in width. Sherman had determined to do his utmost to end the war, and he considered this method a necessary evil. The South was alarmed. The Confederate General Beauregard tried to check Sherman's army, but that veteran army overcame all opposition, and on December 22, 1864, marched into Savannah, which the Confederates had abandoned. Sherman telegraphed to President Lincoln, " I beg to present to you, as a Christmas gift, the city of Savannah."

Sherman's army had marched two hundred and fifty miles from Atlanta to the sea. January 15, 1865, they started north into South Carolina, and soon had added the cities of Columbia and Charleston to their captures. Meantime Grant was gradually overcoming Lee's army in Virginia, and the war was soon brought to a close. Sherman's march through Georgia had contributed greatly to the speedy end of the conflict.

The song "Marching Through Georgia" became one of the most popular of the Union songs of the war. Wherever Sherman's veterans gathered that song was sure to be heard.

MARCHING THROUGH GEORGIA
By Henry Clay Work

Bring the good old bugle, boys, we'll sing another song—
Sing it with a spirit that will start the world along—
Sing it as we used to sing it fifty thousand strong,
    While we were marching through Georgia.

Chorus
    " Hurrah ! Hurrah ! we bring the jubilee !
    Hurrah ! Hurrah ! the flag that makes you free ! "
    So we sang the chorus from Atlanta to the sea,
    While we were marching through Georgia.

How the darkeys shouted when they heard the joyful sound !
How the turkeys gobbled which our commissary found !
How the sweet potatoes even started from the ground,
    While we were marching through Georgia.

Yes, and there were Union men who wept with joyful tears,
When they saw the honored flag they had not seen for years ;
Hardly could they be restrained from breaking forth in cheers
    While we were marching through Georgia.

" Sherman's dashing Yankee boys will never reach the coast ! "
So the saucy rebels said—and 'twas a handsome boast,
Had they not forgot, alas ! to reckon on a host,
    While we were marching through Georgia.

So we made a thoroughfare for Freedom and her train,
Sixty miles in latitude—three hundred to the main ;
Treason fled before us, for resistance was in vain,
    While we were marching through Georgia.

LIX

O Captain! My Captain!

ON April 9, 1865, General Lee surrendered the Army of Northern Virginia to General Grant at Appomattox Court House in Virginia, and practically brought the Civil War to an end. Nine days later, on April 18, 1865, President Lincoln was shot in a theatre in Washington, and died the next day. His assassination was part of a conspiracy, the intention being to kill the President and several of the leading members of his Cabinet; and Secretary of State Seward was wounded on the same evening, but not seriously. The rejoicing at the conclusion of the long war was at once overshadowed by the death of the great man who had overcome such tremendous difficulties and saved the Union. In the space of his term as President Abraham Lincoln had won the loyal devotion of almost all of his fellow citizens, and the tragedy of his assassination made them realize suddenly how much they had trusted to his wise judgment to heal the wounds of war. The nation mourned for Lincoln as for no one else. The greatness of his patriotism had been understood by all.

Walt Whitman's poem was one of the finest expressions of the common sorrow at the loss of a cap-

tain who had brought his ship at last to port, only to
fall on the deck at the moment of victory.

O CAPTAIN! MY CAPTAIN!
By Walt Whitman

O Captain! my Captain! our fearful trip is done ;
The ship has weather'd every rack, the prize we sought is won ;
The port is near, the bells I hear, the people all exulting,
While follow eyes the steady keel, the vessel grim and daring :
   But O heart ! heart ! heart !
   O the bleeding drops of red,
    Where on the deck my Captain lies,
    Fallen cold and dead !

O Captain ! my Captain ! rise ʋp and hear the bells ;
Rise up—for you the flag is flung—for you the bugle trills ;
For you bouquets and ribbon'd wreaths—for you the shores
  a-crowding ;
For you they call, the swaying mass, their eager faces turning ;
   Here, Captain ! dear father !
   This arm beneath your head ;
    It is some dream that on the deck
    You've fallen cold and dead.

My Captain does not answer, his lips are pale and still ;
My father does not feel my arm, he has no pulse nor will :
The ship is anchor'd safe and sound, its voyage closed and done ;
From fearful trip the victor ship, comes in with object won :
   Exult, O shores, and ring, O bells !
   But I, with mournful tread,
    Walk the deck my Captain lies,
    Fallen cold and dead.

LX

Saxon Grit

ROBERT COLLYER, the author of this poem, read it at the New England dinner on December 22, 1879, given in commemoration of the Landing of the Pilgrims. It tells of the strength of the Saxon race, and traces the ancestry of Brother Jonathan in America back through the stirring history of England.

First was Harold, the last Saxon king in England. He succeeded Edward the Confessor on the throne in 1066, but William, Duke of Normandy, disputed his claim, and invaded England with a great army in September of that year. Harold was in the north, fighting invaders from Norway. He won the battle of Stamford Bridge, in Yorkshire, and turned south to meet William. At the battle of Hastings the English army was overwhelmingly defeated, and Harold killed. William the Conqueror became king, and united the Norman race with the Saxon.

Later came Robin Hood, the native outlaw hero, who lived in Sherwood Forest, and with his band of merry men made war on proud Norman nobles who came his way. He is supposed to have lived in the twelfth century, and was as friendly to the poor and oppressed as he was hostile to the rich and powerful.

Afterwards Ket, the tanner, and Wat Tyler, the

smith, both Saxons, led revolts against tyranny. Wat
marched on London in 1381, when Richard II was
king, and although his revolt failed at the time, it
helped to improve the lot of the English peasants.
Ket's rising came much later, in the days when Henry
VIII reigned.

So the Saxon fight for liberty went on through the
ages, and Saxon grit led the Pilgrims to cross the sea
and make a new home for freedom in the western
world. Thus it is that " Brother Jonathan," the son
of old " John Bull," has much the same qualities to-day
that belonged to Harold, and Robin Hood, Ket and
Wat, and all the Saxon blood.

SAXON GRIT

By Robert Collyer

Worn with the battle, by Stamford town,
Fighting the Norman, by Hastings bay,
Harold, the Saxon's, sun went down,
While the acorns were falling one autumn day.
Then the Norman said, " I am lord of the land :
By tenor of conquest here I sit ;
I will rule you now with the iron hand ; "
But he had not thought of the Saxon grit.

*   *   *   *   *   *

To the merry green-wood went bold Robin Hood,
With his strong-hearted yeomanry ripe for the fray,
Driving the arrow into the marrow
Of all the proud Normans who came in his way ;

Scorning the fetter, fearless and free,
Winning by valor, or foiling by wit,
Dear to our Saxon folk ever is he,
This merry old rogue with the Saxon grit.

And Ket, the tanner, whipped out his knife,
And Wat, the smith, his hammer brought down,
For ruth of the maid he loved better than life,
And by breaking a head, made a hole in the Crown.
From the Saxon heart rose a mighty roar,
" Our life shall not be by the King's permit ;
We will fight for the right, we want no more ; "
Then the Norman found out the Saxon grit.

For slow and sure as the oak had grown
From the acorns falling that autumn day,
So the Saxon manhood in thorpe and town
To a nobler stature grew alway ;
Winning by inches, holding by clinches,
Standing by law and the human right,
Many times failing, never once quailing,
So the new day came out of the night.

*   *   *   *   *

Then rising afar in the western sea,
A new world stood in the morn of the day,
Ready to welcome the brave and the free,
Who could wrench out the heart and march away
From the narrow, contracted, dear old land,
Where the poor are held by a cruel bit,
To ampler spaces for heart and hand—
And here was a chance for the Saxon grit.

Steadily steering, eagerly peering,
Trusting in God your fathers came,
Pilgrims and strangers, fronting all dangers,
Cool-headed Saxons with hearts aflame.

Bound by the letter, but free from the fetter,
And hiding their freedom in Holy Writ,
They gave Deuteronomy hints in economy,
And made a new Moses of Saxon grit.

They whittled and waded through forest and fen,
Fearless as ever of what might befall ;
Pouring out life for the nurture of men ;
In faith that by manhood the world wins all.
Inventing baked beans and no end of machines ;
Great with the rifle, and great with the axe—
Sending their notions over the oceans,
To fill empty stomachs and straighten bent backs.

Swift to take chances that end in the dollar,
Yet open of hand when the dollar is made,
Maintaining the "meetin'," exalting the scholar,
But a little too anxious about a good trade ;
This is young Jonathan, son of old John,
Positive, peaceable, firm in the right,
Saxon men all of us, may we be one,
Steady for freedom and strong in her might.

Then, slow and sure, as the oaks have grown
From the acorns that fell on that autumn day,
So this new manhood in city and town,
To a nobler stature will grow alway ;
Winning by inches, holding by clinches,
Slow to contention, and slower to quit,
Now and then failing, never once quailing,
Let us thank God for the Saxon grit.

Glossary

Adamantine : something which cannot be broken.
Augurs : soothsayers.
Barb : a horse noted for spirited action.
Bent, on the bent : on the ground.
Berserk : a warrior or champion of Scandinavia.
Brake : a fern, and a place overgrown with bushes.
Bravo : a ruffian.
Burgess : a citizen with the right to vote.
Burgher : a citizen.
Cannonier : one in charge of a cannon.
Carline : an old woman.
Catch : a rollicking song.
Champaign : open country.
Claymore : a two-handed Scotch sword.
Cloth-yard : a yard-stick to measure cloth.
Cohorts : a body of troops.
Contemners : those who show contempt.
Cormorant : a bird of the sea.
Cornet : the flag of a troop of cavalry.
Corsair : a sea-pirate.
Cowl : a monk's hood.
Cowthie : kindly.
Cuirasse : a piece of armor to protect the body.
Culverin : a type of cannon.
Deuteronomy : a book of the Bible, which contains the second
   giving of the law by Moses.
Devildoms : acts of the Devil.
Disembogue : to empty into.

Don: a nickname for a Spaniard.

Dun: dark.

Duniewassal: a Highland chief.

" *Erin, slanthagal go bragh* ": an Irish watchword, " May Ireland flourish forever ! "

Fallow deer: pale red or yellow deer.

Fen: marshland.

Fleur de lis: the lily that was the emblem of France.

Fold: an enclosure for sheep.

Fustian: a coarse twilled cotton stuff.

Galleon: a large vessel.

Galliard: a lively dance.

Gentile: the heathen, those who did not worship the god of the Jews.

Gerfalcon: a species of falcon.

Gullie: a large knife.

Hale: to draw.

Harpy: a fabulous monster of prey.

Hart: a buck.

Hinds: peasants.

Hireling: one who is hired.

I ween: I think or imagine.

I wis: certainly.

Impearled: set in pearls.

" *In forma pauperis* " : as a poor man.

Inquisition: a Roman Catholic tribunal for punishing heresy.

Kine: cattle.

Kraken: a sea-monster.

Lauwine: an avalanche.

Lea: a meadow.

Leige: lord.

Leman: a wanton woman.

Leviathan: a sea-monster.

Lode: blows.

Lucumo: the Etruscan name for a chief.

Mall: a public walk.

Marrow: a companion.

May: the flower of the hawthorn.

Musqueteer: a man armed with a musket.

Must: the juice of grapes for wine.

Oriflamme: the royal banner of France.

Philabeg: a kilt, or skirt reaching to the knees, worn by Scotchmen.

Pike: a weapon like a spear.

Pinnace: a small sailing-vessel.

Pique: the point of a saddle.

Pistole: a gold coin.

Pleugh: Scotch for plow.

Port: bearing, manner.

Pow: head.

Provost: the mayor of a Scotch city or town.

Quarry: a pile of dead game.

Rack: storm.

Rampired: fortified.

Redoubted: valiant.

Ronde: a stately French dance.

Ruth: pity.

Saga: a Scandinavian legend.

Sapper: a soldier who digs mines.

Scaur: a steep place.

Sea-mew: a gull.

Ships of the line: men-of-war large enough for a line of battle.

"*Sic semper*:" "Sic semper tyrannis" (thus always with tyrants) is the motto of the State of Virginia.

Skald: a Scandinavian poet or bard.

Skoal: a Scandinavian exclamation meaning "Hail!"

Slee: sly.

Slogan: a war-cry.

Southrons: Southerners.

Tale: number or allotment.

Target: a shield.

Thorpe: a Saxon word for a number of farmhouses.

Thumbscrew: an instrument of torture.

Tribune: an officer of Rome.

Truncheon: a staff of office.

Valhalla: the Scandinavian paradise.

Vans: wings.

Viking: a sea-rover or pirate of the Norsemen.

Wassail-bout: a drinking contest.

Wauken: Scotch for waken.

Were-wolf: a legendary animal much like a wolf.

Whig: often used for those who sided with William III of England.

Whigamore: a contemptuous term for a Whig in politics.

Wode: furious.

References to Names

Albinia : a river of Etruria.

Algidus : a mountain-range south of Rome.

Alsatia : one of the low sections of London in the time of Charles I.

Apennine : a mountain range of Italy.

Ashur : Assyria.

Auser : a river of Etruria.

Baal : a heathen god of the Assyrians.

Baltic : a sea of northern Europe, part of the Atlantic Ocean.

Baritarian : Jean Lafitte, a freebooter, had headquarters at Barataria, in Louisiana.

Biscay : a bay on the southwest coast of France.

Blue Ridge : a mountain range of Virginia.

Campania : a district south of Rome.

Carillon : a set of bells playing a melody, a name given to Ticonderoga.

Chickamauga : a river near Chattanooga, Tennessee, where a battle of the Civil War was fought, September 19 and 20, 1863.

Ciminian Hill : a hill in Etruria.

Clanis : a river of Etruria.

Clitumnus : a river of Umbria.

Comitium : a part of the Roman Forum.

Cortona : a city of Etruria.

Cosa : a town of Etruria.

Cossack : a race inhabiting Southern Russia.

Croisickese : a native of La Croisic in Brittany.

Crustumerium : a town in the Sabine country.

Elsinore : a Danish town, north of Copenhagen, where the battle of the Baltic was fought.

Falerii: a town of Etruria.

Forth: an arm of the sea in Scotland, called the Firth of Forth.

Galilee: the sea of Galilee in Palestine.

Hessian: a native of Hesse in Germany.   Many Hessians fought for England as mercenary soldiers in the American Revolution.

Ilva: an island off the Etruscan coast, the modern Elba.

Janiculum: a hill west of Rome.

Juno: a Roman goddess, wife of Jupiter.

Khamsin: a hot southeast wind in Egypt.

Lafayette: a French nobleman who fought for the Colonies in the American Revolution.

Lee: a river of Ireland.

Lorraine: a province of eastern France, a title of the family of Guise.

Malouins: people of St. Malo in Brittany.

Mamilius: a prince of Tusculum in Latium.

Massilia: a Greek colony in Gaul, the modern Marseilles.

Middlesex: a county of Massachusetts near Boston.

Moslem: Mohammedans or Turks.

Mystic: a river that flows into Massachusetts Bay at Boston.

McGregor: a Highland clan.

Nar: a river of Umbria.

Nequinum: a town of Umbria.

Nurscia: probably a god of Clusium.

Ostia: the port of Rome.

Palatinus: one of the hills of Rome.

Pentland: the Pentland hills in Scotland.

Pisæ: a city of Etruria, the modern Pisa.

Populonia: a city of Etruria.

Ramnian: one of the three ruling classes of early Rome.

Riou: a captain of the English navy at the battle of the Baltic.

Rochelle: La Rochelle, a city on the west coast of France.

Salamanca: a city of Spain near which the English defeated the French July 22, 1812.

Santee : a river of South Carolina.

Seville : a city of southern Spain.

Shannon : a river of Ireland.

She-wolf's litter : the Romans, whose founders, Romulus and Remus, were said to have been suckled by a she-wolf.

Shiloh : the battle of Shiloh Church, or Pittsburgh Landing, Tennessee, was fought April 6 and 7, 1862.

Skaw : a cape at the point of Jutland in Denmark.

Skippen : Philip, a major-general of the Parliamentary army.

Solway : an arm of the Irish Sea, part boundary between England and Scotland.

Sutrium : a town of Etruria.

Switzer : a native of Switzerland.

Tarpeian Rock : a high rock in Rome, from which prisoners were thrown.

Tarquin : the family of the early kings of Rome.

Teviotdale : a name often given to Roxburghshire in Scotland.

Thrasymene : a lake of Etruria.

Tifernum : a town of Umbria.

Titian : one of the three ruling classes of early Rome.

Tweed : a river that forms part of the boundary between England and Scotland.

Umbro : a river of Etruria.

Urgo : an island off the Etruscan coast.

Vandal : a member of a Germanic race which captured Rome in 455.

Volaterræ : a city of Etruria.

Volscian : a race south of Rome.

Volsinian mere : a lake of Etruria.

Volsinium : a city of Etruria.

Wallace : a Scotch hero of the thirteenth century in the wars with England.

Westport : the western gate of Edinburgh.

Whitehall : the palace of Charles I in London.